Scottish Review 2009

The annual anthology

Scottish Review 2009

The annual anthology

Edited with an introduction by
Kenneth Roy

ICS Books

First published in Great Britain in 2009
by Institute of Contemporary Scotland
66 John Finnie Street
Kilmarnock KA1 1BS

Copyright 2009 Institute of Contemporary Scotland

ISBN 978 0 9546527 5 3

All rights reserved. No part of this publication may be reproduced, stored in a
retrieval system, or transmitted in any form or by any means, electronic,
mechanical, photocopying, recording, or otherwise, without the prior
permission of the copyright owner.

Printed in Great Britain by the MPG Books Group, Bodmin and King's Lynn

Contents

The foundation of the Scottish Review, in its original print version, was made possible only by the faith and generosity of the following individuals and organisations, all of whom contributed donations before the first edition was published in January 1995:

W R Aitken, Sir Kenneth Alexander, Arthur Anderson, Very Rev Robin Barbour KCVO, MC, Alistair R Brownlie OBE, Rev James Caldwell, Dr Cyril Cohen OBE, Douglas A Connell WS, Dr Iain Cuthbertson, Hon Lord Davidson, John Donachy OBE, George Edwards, Joan P S Ferguson, Medardo Fraile, Tom Gallacher, Tom Gilchrist, Alistair Gracie, James Shaw Grant CBE, Lesley D Grant MBE, John Grieve, Sydney Harrison OBE, Maidie Hart, Alastair Hetherington, William Hunter, David Hutchison, Ian Jack, Andrew Jaspan, Liam Kane, Arnold Kemp, R D Kernohan OBE, Magnus Linklater, Bet Low, Norman Malcolm Macdonald, Vice Admiral Sir Roderick Macdonald, Winifred Macdonald, Dr Farquhar Macintosh CBE, Eric Mackay, Rev Ian Mackenzie, Kenneth F McKeown, Dr John A J Macleod, Professor Malcolm MacLeod, Rt Hon Dr J Dickson Mabon PC, Dr William Manson, Ronald Mavor, George Mitchell (for Grampian Television), Professor R G Mitchell, Alistair Moffat, Peter A Murphy, I M S Park CBE, Dr Tony Paterson, Sir Thomas Risk, George Rosie, The Saltire Society, Scotland The What?, Mr and Mrs J Scott, Scottish Office Information Directorate, Scottish Library Association, Scottish Poetry Library, Scottish Television plc, Rev Dr Henry R Sefton, Allan Shiach, Sheriff G I W Shiach, Isabel L Sinclair QC, Dr Iain Crichton Smith OBE, Sheriff A L Stewart, Ena Lamont Stewart, Professor Alan Thompson, Professor Derick Thomson, Elizabeth Whitley, Rev Laurence Whitley, Donald Whyte JP, Professor Roy Wilkie, Professor Paul Wilkinson, Roy Wilson, William C Wolfe, Rev Canon Kenyon E Wright, Peter D Wright, Tom Wright, Andrew Young, Rt Hon Lord Younger of Prestwick KCVO, TD; and five others who asked to remain anonymous.

Introduction

When the Scottish Review first appeared in 1995, it did so as a 96-page paperback four times a year. It is scarcely credible (at least to me, its founder) that, 14 years later, it is published twice a week as 'Scotland's online current affairs magazine'. Although the internet has devastated the mainstream press, taking away young readers and lucrative sources of advertising, it has created new opportunities for small, independent publishers; we have taken full advantage.

For a little while, we were of a mind to sustain both the print edition (reduced in frequency to twice a year) and the online. This arrangement did not prove to be feasible. Inevitably, limited resources were concentrated on developing the new Scottish Review at the expense of the old. The online version attracts many more readers than the print version ever did and has opened up a wider forum for the discussion of ideas and the sharing of experiences about modern Scotland. Reluctantly, then, we decided to abandon the Scottish Review in its traditional format and devote ourselves to the electronic alternative.

At the same time, however, we hit on a compromise which will keep the magazine alive between familiar covers: an annual anthology bringing together a representative collection of articles from the online editions. This has two principal merits: as a service to those regular readers (including some members of the Institute of Contemporary Scotland, our parent body) who are unconverted to the mixed blessings of the internet; and as a way of prolonging the life of thoughtful journalism. This is the first of the anthologies. It covers a period of 12 months from July

2008 to June 2009 (with the exception of a single piece from early July 2009).

In the way that journalism thrives on bad news, we have been fortunate indeed. When the SR was launched online, the house market was buoyant, unemployment low, and Sir Fred Goodwin a colossus of the financial world. MPs, if not the most popular people in Britain, were generally accorded grudging respect. Labour's hold on such power bases as the east end of Glasgow seemed impregnable. All that changed with shocking abruptness during the course of the Scottish Review's first year online; indeed much of it changed within a few short weeks, as the banks teetered on the brink of collapse. Faithfully twice a week, the Scottish Review has chronicled the end of one Britain and the emergence of a frailer new one. It has also kept an eye on the international scene, devoting much space to the rise and rise of Barack Obama; and, needless to say, it has maintained a critical perspective on Scottish public affairs from a strictly non-party-political standpoint.

As I look back to the list of those whose generous donations prior to publication made possible the establishment of the Scottish Review, I note with sadness how many are dead; in continuing gratitude for their faith in the enterprise, their names are published on a previous page. There is now a new group of supporters to thank: all those contributors, most of them represented in this volume, who write for the magazine without fee because they believe in what we are doing.

Kenneth Roy
Kilmarnock: August 2009

Part I

Money

Money 1

My evening with Sir Fred

Kenneth Roy

Recently, I went for lunch with a man who used to know Fred Goodwin well, socialised with him, held him in high regard. The period of which we talked was long before the fall, a time when Sir Fred was in the ascendancy, not quite master of the universe, his knighthood for services to banking still in the future, but a figure of considerable importance nevertheless.

Naturally I asked my lunch companion the question that anyone in my position would have asked. Was there anything in Fred Goodwin's character, anything in his business methods, hinting at the colossal recklessness to come?

'No,' he replied. 'Absolutely nothing.'

On the contrary, the 'world's worst banker', 'the most hated man in Britain', had once been noted for the steady trajectory of his career and the shrewdness of his judgement. What on earth went wrong? What converted Sir Fred into a modern equivalent of Ibsen's master builder with such terrible consequences for his bank, the UK economy, the reputation of Scotland, and himself?

I should myself have a clue. After all, I am one of the very few journalists ever to have interviewed Fred Goodwin – and a right hash I made of it.

It was a public occasion. The audience consisted mostly of academics, writers and social reformers of various kinds, and as I waited nervously for my first guest of the evening to arrive (for there were several other prominent Scots to follow) I remember thinking that this was not the sort of audience which the chief executive of the Royal Bank of Scotland would find familiar or instinctively sympathetic. There was not a business head among them.

As I say, I waited nervously. Sir Fred and I had not communicated directly before the meeting; all the preliminaries had been handled by his PA. No curiosity about the scope or content of the interview had been expressed. This was unusual.

It could have denoted an arrogance on Sir Fred's part or perhaps simply indifference. Either way it didn't augur well.

Fifteen minutes before the interview was due to begin, he hadn't shown up. One of the organisers frantically phoned his office and was assured he was on his way. He was driving himself, he had left in good time and, worry not, he would be with us at any moment. With barely a minute to spare, he strolled into the meeting room. He was as prompt as the six o'clock news.

Two high stools had been put in place – one for the interviewer, the other for a succession of the great and the good who were to perch upon it. The stools were of a kind you would use to prop up a bar. They were not comfortable for any prolonged period. Sir Fred was not comfortable, but his discomfort had little to do with the informal seating arrangements. He had the demeanour of someone who was wondering what had possessed him to agree to this engagement, what he was doing there, and how soon he could decently leave.

Two things about him struck me at once. He looked incredibly fit and incredibly young. Indeed he was positively boyish in appearance for a man in his late forties, apparently un-careworn by the burdens of running a sprawling, multi-national business. As I appraised the face of the banker, it seemed a face unclouded by tragedy or severe anxiety. But nor did it appear happy – well, not at this moment, not with me, not facing this audience of oddballs. Sir Fred's countenance was wary.

Nor was his interviewer happy. I was displeased with myself for failing to prepare for the interview at all thoroughly. Being more interested in the people I was talking to later in the evening, I had ignored the mere financier, who was virtually unknown outside his own circle. And I was displeased with Sir Fred for his obvious lack of interest and displeased to be told that he would not be staying to hear the other speakers or for dinner afterwards.

In this state of mutual unhappiness, we began.

I did what I often did with awkward customers and started by asking him to describe his father. This technique has been known to break down the most stubborn defences; even so monstrous a personality as John Junor succumbed to it. Fred

Goodwin, however, was petrified by the question – fixed in amazement. From his expression, one could tell that he had never before been asked to describe his father. He had nothing to say about his father or, if he did have something to say, he was not sharing it with Kenneth Roy and his friends. He had very little to say about his childhood in Paisley either. It had been non-eventful, not worth noting on the balance sheet of his life. They had gone on holiday as a family every summer to Girvan. Well, that was a point of contact. I had once lived in Girvan, in a house facing the beach, where young Fred had played as a child. But he had little to say about that either. He had enjoyed his holidays. Yes, they had been all right. Paisley Grammar School, where he was educated? Dismissed in a few monosyllables. The stonewalling Goodwin was becoming an interviewer's nightmare.

And so the impression formed, in so far as any impression formed, of a public figure almost uniquely costive about his personal hinterland; of someone who had, as the saying goes, risen without trace. We stumbled on, but the interview was going nowhere; it might just as well have sunk into the Girvan sands of his otherwise unrecorded boyhood. Only on the subject of money was he relatively animated. He talked with some eloquence, some pride, about the rise of RBS as a global phenomenon, as well he might. But, as the questions from the floor demonstrated, his listeners on this occasion were not impressed by talk of profits. They wished instead to have the speaker's opinion on business ethics and the contribution of the banks to society. Sir Fred responded with growing unease. Pressed to define RBS's responsibilities to the wider community, he referred to the bank's support of rugby. He was greeted with bemusement. Rugby wasn't hacking it. Sports sponsorship wasn't hacking it. Sir Fred wasn't hacking it.

Finally, the poet Tessa Ransford put a killer question that summed up the prevailing mood. 'Sir Fred,' she asked, 'are banks for people or are people for banks?' There was an embarrassed silence and Sir Fred wriggled a little on his high stool. At last he spoke. 'A bit of both, I suppose,' he said weakly. There was no elaboration. A few months ago, when I reminded Tessa Ransford of the occasion, she said she had been provoked to ask the question because she had been so disturbed by the interview. She could claim to be the first person to have rumbled Sir Fred.

On that strange evening, Fred Goodwin should have received an intimation, an early warning, of his own vulnerability. Exposed, as he so rarely was, to a gathering of people who did not accept at face value all he said, whose vision of a decent society was not motivated by profit and growth, he could have engaged with their scepticism. There could have been a genuine dialogue, however tentative. But there was no engagement, no dialogue. He was like a visitor from a distant planet. Unfailingly polite throughout, he left as soon as the interview was over and was succeeded on the high stool by a woman who had gone to prison for her beliefs. We talked brightly of Cornton Vale. It felt like light relief.

'How much do you think the chief executive of a bank is paid?' someone asked me later.

'Oh, I don't know. What do you reckon?'

'Around £75,000 a year?'

3 March 2009

Money 2

House of cards

Walter Humes

Sociologists use the concept of a 'reference group' to explain how people in positions of authority acquire their views and reach decisions. Instead of weighing the evidence dispassionately and subjecting it to careful analysis, powerful players assess what other key individuals think and frame their own response in terms of what they judge will be acceptable to members of the reference group. A form of 'groupthink' develops where nobody has the courage to dissent or take a stance that puts their status at risk. It is a mutually reinforcing process based on consensus, conformity and calculation.

Some of the current financial crisis can be explained in these terms. Investors, financiers and bankers colluded in an exercise which allowed hard selling of dubious products, reckless lending and property inflation. Instead of a solid edifice, they built a house of cards which was bound to collapse sooner or later. Some of them no doubt knew that this was the likely outcome, but a combination of greed and fear kept them going. Nobody had the courage to call the rules of the game into question. Indeed, the leaders were applauded for their wealth-creating 'vision' and rewarded with obscene bonuses and, in a few cases, a little something in the honours list.

It is no accident that all this has occurred at a time when the relationship between staff in high-street banks and ordinary customers has been changed beyond recognition. It has been depersonalised and commodified. This is represented physically in the remodelling of bank interiors where routine transactions (deposits and withdrawals) have been sidelined in favour of the 'real business' of selling new 'goods'. Customers are encouraged to use cash machines and online banking so that the scope for pushing the latest line in bonds or other products is increased. Long-standing clients find themselves dealing with unfamiliar faces who are not interested in everyday pleasantries. All they want is proof of identity and a signature on a form.

Branch bank staff have themselves been downgraded in the brave new world of global finance. They have become merely the front-line workers who are expected to boost sales and reach new targets. The bosses at the top inhabit a different stratosphere, well insulated from the vulgar concerns of ordinary customers. As they glide smoothly from one boardroom meeting to another, viewing sets of figures skilfully massaged by creative accounting, their grasp on reality fades and they begin to believe they are the masters of the universe. In other words, their reference group has created a fantasy world, an illusion easily maintained as they are ushered from luxury hotel suite to limousine to private jet.

Will the fate of Sir Fred Goodwin and the others serve as a much-needed reality check which will prevent future excesses? I rather doubt it. The lessons of history tell us that new reference groups will be formed and different versions of groupthink will emerge. There may be a temporary return to more cautious practices, and gestures towards a tighter regulatory system, but the self-interest of the rich and powerful will soon reassert itself. What may change, however, is the language in which their aspirations are expressed. They will seek to disguise their real intent by playing down the discourse of profit, expansion and enterprise, and polishing up their ethical credentials as responsible global citizens. Don't be fooled.

14 October 2008

Money 3

Basil the bank manager

Alan McIntyre

There are two competing views of human nature. One is that human nature is fundamentally good. This optimism finds expression in the classical liberal view that if the government just got out of the way then everyone would be richer and happier as a result. The alternative view is that human nature is fundamentally flawed. This pessimism (traditionally associated with the utopian left in politics and the Roman Catholic Church in religion), finds expression in the paternalistic view that we need to be protected from ourselves. The broad role of government is to make us play nice for the common good – or in the case of the Vatican to save our eternal souls.

The bankers of the world are now Exhibit A for the prosecution in the case against the traditional liberal viewpoint. Over the last 20 years we deregulated and globalised the financial services industry and apparently ended up breeding a generation of arrogant bankers who thought they were infallible. The direct consequence has been a financial services industry that has gone to hell in a hand basket, closely followed by the rest of the global economy.

So whose fault was it? By all means take Sir Fred's pension away. Good economic incentives like any good religious morality require heaven and hell to be truly effective. But let's not kid ourselves that we're surprised by the bankers' behaviour. Economic history provides absolute clarity that if you offer most people the opportunity to lawfully accumulate vast wealth, then they are going to jump at the chance. Indeed, if we accept that we want to live in a broadly capitalist economy, then this is exactly what we want them to do. Capitalism relies on profit signals to guide behaviour and as Gordon Gekko famously put it in the movie *Wall Street*, 'greed for want of a better word is good' because it helps ensure efficient resource allocation. The bankers of the last 20 years have simply been lab rats in the maze that governments and regulators have designed for them, figuring out the best way to maximise their personal income and amass power and status.

That selfishness, while maybe distasteful to some, was at least predictable. The true scandal is that banking regulators (and the politicians who appointed them) allowed themselves to be seduced by the liberal view of human nature without realising that in the process they were taking the safety catch off weapons of economic mass destruction. When it comes to banking (and a small number of other pastimes such as nuclear energy generation) we forgot that the default setting must be to assume human frailty. This isn't because bankers are any more flawed than the rest of us, but instead because the banking industry itself is special and that uniqueness demands a different and more cautious approach to oversight and regulation.

Banking is different from other businesses in at least three ways. First, it relies on huge amounts of trust and confidence to function effectively. As a depositor you give the bank your money and trust they will pay it back when you need it. As a banker, you trust that the vast majority of those you then lend that money to will also pay it back. If you want to understand the role of trust and confidence in banking just watch Jimmy Stewart as George Bailey in *It's A Wonderful Life*. He stands behind the savings and loan counter in Bedford Falls stopping a run on the bank by patiently explaining that the angry depositors' money isn't in the vault, instead it's in Bob's house, and Frank's house. Unfortunately, there was no George Bailey to stand behind the counter in every Northern Rock branch, only Alistair Darling standing behind the dispatch box like King Canute.

The second unique aspect of banking is leverage. Banking has historically been about borrowing money to make safe bets. If you had £1 to put on an even-money sure thing in the Grand National you'd double your money if it won. If you instead borrowed £10 from your friend in the pub and added it to your £1 bet then you'd make £11, even after paying the £10 back. The problem is of course if you don't win, then you can't expect to have a drink with your friend without the question of the borrowed money coming up. The change over the last 20 years in banking is that rather than borrowing £10 for every £1 of their own money and backing sure things, many of the world's bankers were borrowing anything up to £50 at a time to bet on rank outsiders with a tendency to fall at the first fence.

The final unique and dangerous aspect of banking is its interconnectedness. Money is not only a stand-alone business; it's also the lubricant that greases the wheels of the rest of the economy. Over time the world of finance has also become far more interconnected as capital flows have become global. The consequence has been that if one bank catches a cold, the rest of the financial industry sneezes and the 'real' economy can end up with pneumonia as the supply of credit dries up and the bankers try to save themselves.

What happened over the last 20 years is that regulators and politicians forgot that banking is special and started to treat it like any other industry. Through their tolerance for loose lending practices, higher and higher leverage, and a reliance on caveat emptor instead of active regulation, they allowed the whole system to over-extend itself to the point where one tug on a loose thread (in this case the US mortgage market) caused an evaporation of trust, a seizing up of the global financial markets and economic collateral damage from Beijing to Reykjavik. In the process, the banker as Captain Mainwaring from *Dad's Army* – pompous but ultimately conservative – has morphed into the banker as Basil Fawlty. The centuries-old reputation of Scottish bankers as canny risk managers has also been destroyed. Only HSBC, a Scottish bank in all but name, will survive this crisis with any semblance of dignity.

The pendulum will now swing back. We'll relearn that banking is special and that it really isn't the right place to be experimenting with unfettered capitalism. But as we reregulate it's critical that we do so with intelligence and insight and try to avoid cheap political grandstanding. If you just redesign the maze the rats will figure it out pretty quickly. We need oversight that keeps pace with financial innovation and recognises systemic risk when it starts to appear. Specifically we need to accept that – as much as it goes against free market sensibilities – we need to be able to prick asset bubbles like the housing market before they get out of control. We also need to put in effective firewalls that prevent the propagation of the type of panic we've seen over the last couple of years when even the smart regulators miss something (as they inevitably will). Were the senior bankers of the last 20 years generally arrogant, over-compensated, and deluded that their alchemy was creating real wealth? Absolutely. Were they malicious robbers of widows and orphans? Bernie Madoff aside, generally not. They were simply acting rationally and lawfully within the boundaries that had been set for them.

The real blame lies with the governments and regulators who forgot that the rules of the game in banking need to be very different and – like the Vatican – the most prudent course is to assume the worst about human nature and act accordingly.

26 March 2009

Money 4

The silence of Edinburgh

Kenneth Roy

The centre of Edinburgh is an address unknown to the tourist. It is 86 Princes Street, the New Club, the home of the capital's establishment, a place to 'relax from the hectic pace of modern life', but only if you are fairly important and, for most practical purposes, male. Women are excluded from lunch in the members' dining room, except on Sunday when mixed company is permitted. If you doubt that these antiquated rules apply in the early years of the 21st century, check the club's website.

Nine years ago, when I was raising money to start an educational charity, I became familiar with the New Club as an occasional guest. I was invited there by two venerable institutions to explain myself. Of course the invitation was not put in these rough terms, but the intentions became all too clear. The emissary of the first venerable institution suggested that, since the charity I was trying to establish would merely duplicate its own activities, I should do the decent thing, stop fund-raising and hand over the cash already committed. My lack of enthusiasm for this proposal must have been transparent; an awkward lunch followed.

From the second venerable institution, three emissaries were sent to greet me. A chilly civility prevailed as the chief emissary asked who was intended to benefit from the new charity. 'The young and the poor,' I replied frankly. The atmosphere lifted at once. 'The young and the poor,' echoed the chief emissary in tones of some astonishment. There was a ripple of laughter. It seemed that I was no longer considered a threat; I was merely some harmless eccentric from the west. Lunch on that occasion was amiable, if dull.

Meetings of that sort take place in the New Club all the time. It may promote itself as a place set apart from the 'hectic pace of modern life', but in reality it is an integral part of it, a meeting ground for the powerful and influential to exchange nods and winks in a rarefied atmosphere. It is all very Edinburgh, too; polite, discreet, a bit smug and self-satisfied. Nine years ago, however, the Edinburgh establishment had reason to be smug and self-satisfied. It seemed that a glittering future was assured, a future based on financial services, the handling of other people's money being widely accepted as the means to a prosperous, clean economy.

I remember meeting one of the city's leading bankers. He was full of enthusiasm for the idea of an independent Scotland with a low tax regime, 5% or 10% lower than England's, encouraging back to Scotland those money-minded, kilted expats whom he had recently observed at a Burns night in Hong Kong, passing round Scottish song books and shouting them out at the tops of their voices, standing on their chairs as they did so. 'Dammit,' he had thought, 'why aren't these people in Scotland?' When I expressed some scepticism about this exciting vision of a brave new Scotland, the banker insisted that the financial sector was already a big employer, could become very much bigger still, and was the way to go. The financiers who stood on the chairs in Hong Kong belting out patriotic ditties were never lured back; we are still waiting for independence and the low tax regime. But otherwise my friend the banker saw his prophecy fulfilled. Edinburgh did indeed go for financial services. We have lived to witness the results.

In the preliminary stages of the banking collapse – played out in the distant month of October 2008 – the Scottish dimension of the scandal was more easily obscured. The acronyms helped. HBOS – it was easy to forget that this was once the proud Bank of Scotland. RBS – it could stand for anything or, as it turned out, nothing. In England it took quite a while to work out that this too disguised the word Scotland. More recently, however, particularly since the popular outcry over Sir Fred's pension, a change in terminology has been detectable. It is now more common for television commentators to drop RBS in favour of the full, unclothed Monty. The Cockney chap from the Evening Standard, often to be found on the BBC's breakfast-time sofa, is particularly fond of stressing the word Scotland in the title of the failed bank. It is irritating but, unhappily, it is true.

The blow to Edinburgh's self-esteem is devastating. Where

does the city go from here? It seems unable to organise a tram system, never mind a functioning bank. But the assault is wider in its grievous impact. It infects all of Scotland: to those outside, perhaps to many inside, we now look and feel like a small, rather silly country, once noted for financial prudence, which went soft in the head with its big ideas. We might as well face up to the abrupt decline in our national reputation and attempt something in the nature of a mature discussion about its causes and consequences.

Yet an odd thing is happening or, rather, not happening. There has been no mature discussion, indeed scarcely any discussion mature or otherwise; the intelligent life of the country has been paralysed into silence; one imagines that, in the New Club, they are reduced to appalled whispers.

At an obvious level, the silence is comprehensive. The non-executive directors of RBS, who agreed to the calamitous acquisition of the Dutch bank and signed off Sir Fred's pension package, have said nothing. The auditors have said nothing. Sir Fred himself, beyond his obligatory appearance before the Treasury select committee, has said nothing, disappearing from view for the time being, perhaps forever. The more shadowy characters behind the HBOS fiasco have said nothing. Sir James Crosby, the banker turned regulator, has said nothing. There may be reasons why the central characters are saying nothing, reasons we can only guess at, but the silence of what is loosely called 'civil society' is less explicable. The most important event in Scotland for years – the distintegration of its independent banking system – has been widely reported as a financial and political story, but virtually unanalysed as a wider cultural phenomenon.

The most deafening silence of all is to be heard at Holyrood. In October 2008, when the scandal broke, the First Minister was relatively voluble on the subject. He blamed HBOS's troubles on spivs and speculators. This belief was not widely shared. He was then questioned on television about RBS, where he had worked (between 1980 and 1987) as an economist. His interviewer, Jon Sopel, asked him if Sir Fred Goodwin should remain as chief executive. 'Let's let the people in charge guide these institutions into safer times and let's get behind that effort,' Mr Salmond replied. This was among the more ringing endorsements of Sir Fred, perhaps the only one, generous in all the circumstances, but once again there was little agreement.

Since then, the First Minister has been uncharacteristically muted about Sir Fred in particular and the destruction of our main financial institutions in general. When the possibility of a belated Scottish parliamentary inquiry into the scandal was briefly discussed only last week, Mr Salmond said that he would support such an inquiry only if it dealt with the 'deplorable practices across the banking sector' – a qualification neatly avoiding Scottish culpability. Suddenly, those reserved powers have been found to be terribly convenient in the most unexpected way.

Nuffink to do with us, guv? The main players operated from Edinburgh, the most grandiose schemes were hatched in Edinburgh, the worst decisions were made in Edinburgh. All this is inescapable; all this has to be confronted one day. But one suspects it won't be soon. Now that the 'hectic pace of modern life' has finally caught up with our capital city, everyone's gone into hiding.

10 March 2009

Part II

Life

Life 1

Zone of humiliation

Gordon MacGregor

It is perhaps axiomatic that a party whose name is a synonym for work should see wage labour as an almost spiritually redeeming activity. As Harriet Harman, minister for social security, trilled in 1997: 'Work is central to the government's attack on social exclusion. Work is the only route to financial independence. But it is also much more. Work is not just about earning a living. It is a way of life...work helps to fulfil our aspirations – it is the key to independence, self-respect and opportunities for advancement.'

Given the centrality of work to this government in combating social exclusion, I recently approached my local 'buroo' in the radiant expectation that I would be greeted by helpful and motivated staff eager to help me in my struggle towards the working 'way of life'. However, my suspicion that all was not for the best was first aroused when I barrelled through the door into a security guard who demanded that I hand in my umbrella 'for my safety and theirs'. Perhaps my eyes betrayed a spark of Blairite zeal or violent menace. Perhaps I had been muttering Arbeit Macht Frei under my breath. Either way, I was not to be allowed in until I had divested myself of anything dangerous and had publicly stated my business.

My female companion, having no valid reason to accompany me (moral support was a non-starter), was ordered to remain outside. I tried to tell myself that this was simply a by-product of equality: the guards – unable to discriminate – must treat all at the level of the most suspicious and unstable.

Unfortunately, this was merely the first step into a dark region which, while it goes under the name 'JobCentrePlus', might better be described as the 'Zone of Humiliation'. Having negotiated the phalanx of uniformed thugs I was directed to wait in a queue where I would be required to publicly state my business for a second time to the inner circle of the 'truth and reconciliation' commission. A further gaggle of guards congregated, listening to each plea and smirking to each other on hearing the stumbling supplications of prospective jobseekers as they attempted to negotiate the protocol.

At this point I began to suspect that an almost deliberate logic seemed to be at play which creates frustration. One elderly gentleman, whose giro had not arrived, was told that he could get a replacement but would have to phone an 0845 number in Bathgate. He complained that he didn't have a phone, let alone a mobile, and asked to use the job centre's 'free phones' to call. This was verboten. What was he to do then? Perhaps, the clerk condescended, the Citizens' Advice Bureau might help.

After negotiating the first line of defence I was directed to the inner sanctum, a world of bulging cushions, playgroup fonts and primary colours like some teletubby psikhushka. But the humiliation did not cease.

A young woman, possibly agoraphobic, who seemed to be in some distress, tried to swallow a tablet which became stuck in her throat. Choking, she asked the security guard if she could use the toilet and was smugly informed that none was available for customers. Perhaps a glass of water? She was primly told that the guard had 'no authority' to provide one. She then went to sit beside her friend who was being interviewed by an advisor and was informed that she must sit on a seat three feet away unless she had legitimate business in the office. Every plea stymied, every movement policed, she seeped bleakly into a chair, head on chest, choking on another tranquiliser. The whole time, security circled, searching for minor infractions, directing 'customers' exactly where to sit, chiding them for their use of mobile phones, their failure to embrace the wonderful world of social inclusion.

The impression given is that the job centre has become a criminogenic space, its degrading frustrations and bitter reverses fuelling anger and violence, its 'customers' (as if they have a market choice) the feckless, the addicted and the criminal. If work brings dignity then being unemployed is to be stripped of dignity. At no time is the jobseeker allowed to forget that he is something less than fully a citizen. The staff (for the most part) seemed helpful and cheery, struggling with the system as much as their 'customers' and unable to use discretion at any point. But for most who find themselves in the job centre there seems to be a stoic resignation that this is about anything but 'jobseeking'. Rather it is a ritual of humiliation, resurrecting something of the vindictiveness of the Victorian workhouse.

However, this may be a less comfortable conceit now that many of the middling (or to use the new term, 'aspirant') classes are finding themselves on the dole queue. They too will find themselves having to justify the economic heresy of not working. But they need not worry for the job centre now offers a plethora of fascinating careers. In Govan, for instance, where once a man could only look to the rewards of heavy industry at Brown's shipyard or Kvaerner, opportunities for advancement now abound as a sandwich artist (sic), 'befriender', or even the cheery Victorian toil of a gutter cleaner (must have own ladder).

But while work is touted as a panacea for all modern ills we reserve our unbridled malice for those who – God forbid – may be getting something for nothing. Benefit-supplemented work, however poorly paid, however unsafe and un-unionised, however long the hours, is positively criminal. This attitude can be seen in the adverts: a morbidly obese woman supplants her meagre income by the drudgery of ironing another family's clothes, unaware that a surveillance team from the DHSS are on her tail. The adverts seem to operate on the glib assumption that we would all wish to see this 'cheat' broken on the wheel and end with the warning that 'we're closing in'. Perhaps we dislike the unemployed and the lumpen because they remind us how precarious our own existence is.

It never fails to amuse that these folk devils are so ruthlessly hunted for their petty infractions at a time when bankers have wantonly trashed the country's economy. In retributionist America they would face the prospect of an orange jumpsuit and federal accomodation. In China the response would be more robust. But this country has lost the ability to hold to account in any meaningful way. And so, like frustrated brutes, we must simply kick the dog...or the unemployed.

3 March 2009

Life 2

Tunnel of hate

Islay McLeod

The stink of sectarianism is again rife after the first Old Firm match of the season. The idea abroad – literally abroad – of an evil mass taunting an opposing sea of innocents is preposterous. I was there at Parkhead that day and saw and heard something very different.

Unknowingly, I happened to walk to the stadium along the route allotted to Celtic supporters. Ugly metal fences had been erected, segregating supporters on either side of a barren no man's land. Surrounded by thousands of green and white clad bodies, I was reassured by the general mood of joviality. Even as they entered the grounds of Celtic Park, the fans were still amiable, grabbing snacks and queuing up for tickets. The police were relaxed and unperturbed, though it did sicken me to see that their steeds had plastic visors fixed over their eyes.

Trouble started in the tunnel – an outrageously narrow, dark space lined with turnstiles, Celtic supporters being swept through from both directions. It was there that behaviour changed dramatically and chants erupted. Instantly I felt threatened. Deafening songs laced with obscenities and the lines 'Go hame ya huns' and 'God bless the Pope' came blasting out. The noise reverberated on surrounding walls, louder and louder. Many in the tunnel sang, not the minority we are often led to believe. Young children were present, silently being conditioned by the 'responsible' adults around them – another generation poisoned.

Feeling dizzy, I stumbled through, knocked this way and that by unapologetic bodies. A reek of alcoholic breath and wet concrete lingered in the cramped space. Hostility was directed towards events staff by ticket-less or drunken fans denied entry. Glad to reach the other end and fresh air, I headed towards the opposite side of the no man's land, to the opposition. The mood there was more sombre. The odd shout about 'getting rid of the fenians' was audible, with one fan attempting a solo *Rule Britannia*. Yet policing was more stringent with all tickets checked before anyone could pass through the outer gates.

An anti-Irish chant about the potato famine sung by Rangers supporters during the match has provoked the Irish government to voice its concern. The club's response has been pathetic – a website post claiming that Rangers are being 'targeted' while other perpetrators are ignored. True, less has been said about the Celtic goalkeeper who openly taunted opposing fans. Less still, if anything, about the confrontational atmosphere outside the ground.

But let's get one thing clear – both sides are the problem. Sectarianism is division. Division stopping conversation. Division making solution impossible. Our approach is like the tunnel, narrow and one-sided. These disgusting chants which made me feel so unnerved and threatened cannot be policed during games. The second the whistle is blown for kick-off, it's too late. The curse of sectarianism has to be solved outside the stadium – in streets and houses all over Scotland. The human behaviour I witnessed in the tunnel suggests that when caged in a tight space, we turn to aggression and intimidation. Inside the stadium is even worse, with opposing fans facing each other – triggering taunts and reactions.

There is no immediate panacea for this disease. But I'm clear about one thing – I have no plans to return to an Old Firm game until one is found.

19 September 2008

Life 3

Caught on a train

Walter Humes

I do not normally travel first class on trains but it was a longish trip (Birmingham and back in one day) and I had managed to get a keen price by booking online. The relative comfort and quiet would, I anticipated, enable me to prepare for my meeting. I managed to get the work done quite quickly and then turned my attention to my fellow passengers.

Most of them conformed to expectations. There were business types, women travelling on their own, a few elderly folk. One passenger, however, was quite different. He was big, bald and beefy, wearing a black tee-shirt and jeans. Beefy (as I shall call him) ignored the free copy of the Times on offer and settled down with the sports pages of his Daily Record.

After a while he put this aside and extracted two books from his suitcase. One was a biography of Ally McCoist, the other a study of Glasgow criminals. The latter helped me to decide that it might not be wise to engage him in witty badinage in case an ill-judged quip led in an unwelcome direction (the casualty department of the nearest hospital). This was reinforced when he received several calls on his mobile from guys with names like Shug and Benny. The callers all Inquired after Beefy's health. He assured them he was 'brand new' but kept the calls short, explaining that he was on a train and would ring them later. By now my imagination was working overtime and I had visions of a network of gangsters planning a bank heist or a drugs deal.

I wandered along to the buffet in search of refreshment (a steward service in the first-class carriage was available only after Preston). Here I discovered an important class distinction. A passenger paying the standard fare who asked for a bacon roll would receive a big coarse version of this delicacy. But a first class passenger would receive a breakfast pack with a much daintier finger roll, a small pot of yogurt and a pack of fresh apple slices. Clearly the train company operated on the principle that first-class passengers were likely to be health conscious while the rest would be happy to clog their arteries with cholesterol, however much to their heart's discontent.

Back in the carriage, the steward service duly arrived and Beefy was surprisingly picky about his food. He was disappointed that Irn Bru was not on offer. Instead of the liquid nectar made from girders, he had to settle for Diet Coke. The sandwiches did not please him either and the steward was bold enough to ask 'Are you on a special diet?' I was tempted to venture 'A fish supper and deep-fried Mars bar diet perhaps?' but my survival instinct ensured that my lips remained firmly buttoned.

The homeward journey was much less interesting. The carriage was full and overheated, with self-important executives parading their laptops. At Crewe a group of four young men joined the train and proceeded to bore the rest of the company with boastful talk of their sporting exploits. I found it hard to concentrate on the crime novel I was reading, even though I had by now started to identify one of the main characters with Beefy. By the end of the journey I rather missed his menacing presence. I bet he could have reduced the young loudmouths to silence with a single glance. There's something to be said for having a Rottweiler in first-class.

27 November 2008

Life 4

The big snow

Jock Gallagher

On Monday the television doomily reported that London was paralysed. No buses, no tubes, no trains...and threw in for good measure that conditions underfoot made walking beyond perilous. When I decided to ignore all this and set off for London in the middle of the afternoon my wife looked at the leaden sky and said simply but possibly accurately: 'You're mad!'. I told myself that the mileage from my home in Worcestershire to central London is a mere 120 miles. Besides, in my mind, my journey really was necessary.

I have spent the best part of a year setting up the launch of the Centre for Freedom of the Media at London's Chatham House. We had set up a half-day conference to look at what had become of media freedom in the 20 years since the fall of the Berlin Wall. There were guest speakers from Berlin, Vienna, Moscow and Kiev. The expected audience included senior journalists from the British and Russian media, academics from 10 universities, diplomats from several embassies, lawyers and politicians. The Chatham House people – partners in the conference – had had nearly 200 acceptances and were nearly as expectant as me about an important occasion. So I had a fair incentive to be there regardless of the weather.

When I ploughed my way through about four inches of snow to the station, I was disturbed to find that the car park was deserted. There was no one on the platform and when I went to the ticket office, the booking clerk shook his head gloomily: 'London? You'll be lucky!'. He seemed reluctant to sell me the ticket, almost as if he expected to have to sort out a refund when the train failed to materialise. It did although it was late...by two minutes. Surprise, surprise, there was no buffet car.

It's a circuitous route that takes us tortuously north-west through the Black Country to Birmingham before we're allowed to then turn south-east for the capital. All along the route the snow was piled high and every now and again the flurry of snow would turn to blizzard. The Chiltern Railways heating actually worked, which allowed the view to appear very picturesque. Somewhere along the way the conductor was pleased to announce we had picked up the two late minutes. Three hours later we arrived in London – exactly on time.

It was only as I tried to go out of Marylebone Station that the chaos that is London became clear. There was no queue for taxis. There were no taxis. There was no queue for buses. There were no buses. This was five o'clock in the evening at what should have been the rush hour. There was no rush hour.

No attempt had been made to clear the pavements and in the evening's sub-zero temperature, the slush had turned to glistening ice. Shrewdly, as it turned out, I had booked a hotel less than a mile from the station. It took me only about 15 minutes to glide gracefully across the ice and although I had the odd hairy moment, I didn't once lose my balance. Later on television I did see those unfortunates crashing down the stairs at Victoria Station.

I did lose my cool, however, when I hit the hotel. They weren't expecting me. They didn't think anyone would have made it from the north. My room had been given to a stranded London businessman. Just before I could explode or even brandish the confirmation email, they went into diplomatic mode and said they would of course fit me in elsewhere and would adjust the bill. My new room proved to be a box on the second floor – it was initially unheated. The double bed (which I always book) was a single reminiscent of my old army bunk and the bath was a shower with no soap. They soon sorted the heating and supplied soap – I think I was meant to be grateful that they had put themselves out.

Later, on the deserted street, I failed to find a black cab and retreated to the hotel and put myself at the mercy of the dreaded mini-cab system. The journey that would normally have cost about £8 cost me £20 and took me through what was by now a ghost city. Restaurants were closed and so were the theatres and cinemas. There were very few pedestrians and almost as few cars.

When I got to the reception laid on at a colleague's home, the difference between the Londoner and the non-Londoner couldn't have been more marked. Those who had travelled from Berlin and Moscow, as well as Worcestershire and Sheffield, were totally sanguine and said little of their journeys. However those who came from different areas around London spoke breathlessly of miserable journeys, near misses and of their anxiety about getting back home.

Throughout most of Monday, my email and then my mobile phone brought grim news about the likelihood of the conference being cancelled. With Heathrow closed, our international speakers were unlikely to reach London. Even if they did, Chatham House was unlikely to be able to stage the conference. Only a handful of their staff had made it to work on Monday and that day's conference crashed. The fear was that Tuesday would be a grim action replay.

I was never once tempted to call it quits and blame it all on the weather. We found alternative venues and prepared for a truncated version. Then the tide turned. A speaker from Moscow rang from her London hotel and asked the time of the reception. She had arrived at Heathrow totally unaware of any problems. Two other Russians reported in shortly afterwards. Our man from Berlin had one flight cancelled but simply sat it out at the airport and came on the next plane. We had a sad call from Kiev where the Ukrainian journalist had been told flights to Heathrow had been cancelled. He checked out the possibilities of flying from Kiev to Amsterdam, going by train to Paris and catching the Eurostar to London only to find that the London terminus was closed. He was our only casualty.

Then came good news – Chatham House confirmed they would certainly muster enough staff to handle the conference although they were uncertain about being able to provide their usual hospitality. When Tuesday came, we gathered all the speakers and a few key guests in the reception room at Chatham House and apologised for lunch appearing in the form of sandwiches. No one minded.

Ten minutes before we were due to start, I looked into the conference room and got a shock. There were six people luxuriating in the 200 seats. It appeared that the worst had happened. The weather had beaten us. Before I could report back to my colleagues, however, a few more people arrived...and then some more...and some more. 'People often leave it until the last minute,' said the Chatham House events manager. When we took in the speakers, they were warmly welcomed by an audience of around 140 brave souls. The freedom of the media isn't going to be impeded by the hysteria of the London-centric media.

5 February 2009

Part III

Society

Society 1

Silence and fear at the barber's

Kenneth Roy

On the day that the Lockerbie bomber, as he is usually described, was refused bail pending his long-delayed appeal, I happened to be visiting a barber's shop near the office. Two members of the staff were discussing the judicial decision and his terminal illness. There was unanimous support for the former, no sympathy for the latter.

'If it was left to me,' said one of the hairdressers, a woman in her twenties, 'I'd...'

The rest was crude; vicious. She was, however, exercising her right to freedom of speech. The customers – the shop was fairly busy – were either blank and uncomprehending or silently acquiescent; it was difficult to tell which. But clearly no dissent was expected, otherwise why would the staff have been so relaxed about sharing their views with the rest of the room? Perhaps they were arrogant enough to assume a consensus. If they did, they assumed wrongly about at least one of their punters.

I sat frozen to the spot. For a few seconds, I could scarcely believe the evidence of my own ears. Had she really said that? In front of customers? When I'd recovered my composure – although I was still trembling with anger – I stood up and addressed the shop. I said that I strongly objected to the sentiments expressed, and added that Abdelbaset Ali Mohmed al Megrahi might well be completely innocent, that there was more than enough doubt to justify the appeal, and that the Scottish judicial system had behaved with shaming inhumanity in continuing to detain him in prison.

Of course I knew I was wasting my breath. The prejudice in the back-street of this small Scottish town was too deep to be softened. But at least I had spoken up; I too had exercised my right to freedom of speech.

There is a flaw in the last two paragraphs: more than a flaw:

there is a lie. It is true that I was trembling with anger. True that the views I have just stated are the views I genuinely hold. But the rest is fabrication. I did not stand up and address the shop. I stayed where I was until it was my turn. 'Next please' – the curt imperative of a woman at the back of the shop who had not taken part in the original exchange. I went over and had my hair cut. She did not speak to me and I did not speak to her. I looked in the mirror and stared reproachfully at my own reflection.

Why had I not challenged this affront?

Was it apathy? Surely not. I feel strongly about the case. Three of the most outstanding people I have ever met - Robert Black (emeritus professor of Scots law at Edinburgh University), Jim Swire (father of one of the victims) and Tam Dalyell (the most tenacious parliamentarian of the modern era) – have all studied the evidence, Bob Black in the most scrupulous and sustained detail, and are either emphatic in declaring Megrahi innocent or have serious doubt about his guilt. We are almost certainly witnessing a tragic miscarriage of justice.

If not apathy, then what? Why did I not speak out, if only to satisfy my own conscience? Why did I let these people away with it? There is a psychological theory that individuals, confronted with the apparent integrity of a group, in this case of seven or eight people, will conform rather than take a stand. There is a simple word to describe this theory and the word is fear. I was afraid of what might happen to me if I uttered the words in my heart; afraid of being ridiculed or humiliated; afraid of the wrath of the group. It was so much easier to say nothing, to leave without confrontation or nastiness. I must go on being a part of this community, after all.

Then I thought of other barber's shops in other places, at other times. I thought of barber's shops in pre-war Germany, thought of myself in the back street of a small town just like this one, and of the anti-semitism in the air, and wondered what I would have done in those extreme circumstances. I didn't like the answer I was getting from the reflection of myself in the mirror. If I could not find a word to say in support of a dying man in a Scottish prison cell, when there was no obvious risk to my physical well-being or livelihood, what were the chances that I would have defended my Jewish friends in pre-war Germany?

'In 1942,' wrote Anne-Marie Bunting, 'a unit of ordinary, middle-aged German reserve policemen were ordered to kill all the inhabitants of a Polish village. Most of these men had never fired a shot at a human being, yet they killed with little hesitation and would go on to slaughter thousands more in cold blood...Although subject to anti-semitic propaganda, these men were not ideologically indoctrinated to kill Jews, nor were they career Nazis, nor had they become brutalised by combat.'

Anne-Marie Bunting discussed the case of reserve police battalion 107, and its abrupt descent into barbarism, in her winning paper in the 2005 Young UK and Ireland Programme. She went on: 'I could not be certain that I would have taken a stand. I did not know whether I had instincts similar to the men of batallion 107, nor whether I would have had the clarity of thought or strength of character to resist those instincts had I been in Germany in 1942...What were my morals? What did I value and what would I fight for?'

It would be foolish to imagine that, in minor ways, these questions do not press down on us in the daily routine of our relatively unthreatened, relatively peaceful, democratic society. They pressed down on me in that barber's shop. I went in for a haircut. I left doubting my own moral character.

To echo Anne-Marie Bunting: 'What do I value and what would I fight for?' Free speech, perhaps? Liberty of thought and expression? Would I value those enough to fight for them? Yes, above all things. But if I value them so much, why did I remain silent?

18 November 2008

Society 2

A teacher's dilemmas

Alex Wood

I recently had brought to my attention the allegation that a third year male student had called a girl in his class 'a whore'. My instant reaction, shared by the depute was, it's never acceptable, he's out. The boy's reaction however took us aback. 'No,' he said, 'I shouldn't have said that in school but there was no harm meant. It's just how we speak to each other.' His rationale for his behaviour notwithstanding, we excluded him.

Despite a lifetime in education I'm not always entirely familiar with the latest nuances of youth culture. Could this, I wondered, be an affectionate term in rap vocabulary? (I confess that when I first heard the phrase 'pimp my ride' I entirely misunderstood its import. I won't share with you the interpretation I erroneously put on it.) At home I checked with my reliable ambassador to teenage thinking, my 18-year-old daughter. Her reaction was instantaneous. Girl to girl, among close friends, in private, it might just be a term of humorous jest. Male to female, never acceptable. In public, always insulting. My initial judgement was confirmed. Interestingly, my depute had, quite separately, checked with her teenage daughter. The response had been identical.

The next week, another incident tested our reactions. A very irate parent was demanding to see me, the headteacher, insisting that she would speak to no-one else. I had seldom seen someone in school so close to tears, so angry. On the Friday evening her daughter had been in the local park with friends. They had met another group of students whom they knew. One of them offered her daughter a drink of juice. She took the bottle, drank and vomited as she realised that she had been given a bottle of urine. To cap the cruelty, she was then inundated by e-mails ridiculing her. The mother wanted action against the perpetrator and those who had been electronically ridiculing her daughter.

The second part was relatively easy. The mother was informed that the e-mailers would be pulled in and well warned that any repetition of their behaviour would see them dealt with harshly. The major offence however, committed well outside school grounds and time, was essentially a police matter. Fortunately, despite the absurd arguments of my own union's vice-president, we have a police officer on campus. Within 20 minutes she was with the mother and daughter, both reassuring and promising action. She then followed through on her promise.

Two cases seemingly satisfactorily addressed: except that the same lad was the perpetrator of both offences. He is not the product of poverty or of a family in crisis. He might, more accurately, be seen as symptomatic of a culture which has lost its ethical perspective. The recent events involving Jonathan Ross and Russell Brand should remind us that a society which pays megabucks for the public humiliation of others can hardly be surprised when that culture becomes the norm in wider circles.

18 November 2008

Society 3

Down with dons?

Walter Humes

Over a period of more than 30 years I have worked as an academic in four Scottish universities – two 'ancient', one granted university status in the 1960s, and one 'post-1992' institution. In all of them I have been fortunate to work alongside able colleagues and interesting students from a wide variety of backgrounds.

Inevitably, the university sector has been subject to many changes during this time. Student numbers have expanded enormously, costs have rocketed, and expectations of the social and economic benefits have risen. New regimes of accountability have been introduced, reflected in the demands of the Scottish Funding Council, the Quality Assurance Agency and the research assessment exercise, all of which seek to ensure that universities are run efficiently and that their standards and output justify the level of public investment that they receive.

Unsurprisingly, these trends have been influenced by the dominant political ideology, which tends to view knowledge as just another 'commodity' to be marketed and exploited commercially: thus universities are increasingly expected to align their activities to the economic priorities of government. This process, it is argued, calls for a much more 'professional' approach to the management of universities, one in which the skills of a range of 'experts' (in finance, information technology, planning, human relations, estates and buildings, and corporate marketing) have assumed growing importance.

However, the central activity of universities – the raison d'etre which justifies their existence – remains the learning and teaching of students. I am in no doubt that, despite all the monitoring that now takes place, the education I received as an undergraduate in the 1960s was immeasurably better than that received by many students today. This is partly because staff-student ratios have not kept pace with the expansion: I received a degree of individual attention (through small tutorial groups and personal feedback on essays) that is no longer possible. But it is not simply a question of the scale of modern universities.

In the 1960s there was a tradition that professors lectured to first year undergraduate classes, on the grounds that students deserved to hear some of the most interesting thinkers in their discipline. This is much less common today. The importance attached to research means that many professors have few teaching commitments: an increasing amount of 'routine' teaching is given to junior staff (some on fixed-term contracts) and even to doctoral students. Junior staff themselves are under pressure to secure research grants and produce research output if they wish to secure tenure, and so they have less time to prepare their lectures than used to be the case. Of course, a great deal of lip service is paid to the importance of teaching 'quality' and QAA engages in elaborate exercises which seem to provide evidence in support of this claim, but I am not alone in doubting whether such exercises would stand up to rigorous research scrutiny by genuinely independent observers. The production of vast amounts of documentation, however well-presented, is no guarantee that good teaching is taking place.

Underlying all of this is a deeper issue about the prevailing culture of many universities. Academic departments are now heavily constrained by the requirements of those 'experts' I referred to earlier (in planning, human resources, corporate marketing, etc). A significant proportion of lecturers' time is taken up with producing returns (often at very short notice) to satisfy the central bureaucratic machine, a machine that has an insatiable appetite: the more it is fed, the more it demands.

In a very real sense, universities are now over-managed in bureaucratic terms and under-led in intellectual terms. This is not surprising, since some of those now appointed to senior management positions do not have a particularly strong academic background. They are judged to have other talents of benefit to the 'corporate' aims of the organisation. These 'corporate' aims place more value on uniform systems and structures than on critical thinking or intellectual independence. This helps to create a climate in which 'groupthink' prevails and anyone who does not subscribe to the prevailing orthodoxies is seen as a dissident. Academic freedom can easily become a casualty in this process.

It would, however, be an over-simplification to see lecturers and professors simply as victims of oppressive managerialism and the growing power of service departments. They must accept some responsibility for what has happened. Their response to the trends I have described has been weak and ineffective. Some have tried to hark back to an imagined golden age of 'donnish dominion', in which they could more or less do as they pleased. That is simply not a credible option in the age of mass higher education. They need to defend the intellectual values that really matter (truth, freedom, integrity) while engaging with the realities of the current situation. They need to recapture the ground they have lost at the main academic forum – the senate – in their own institutions. Senates used to be places where real academic discussion took place: in recent years they have become mere rubber stamps for decisions that have already been agreed elsewhere.

Academics also have to be more outward-looking. Their role as public intellectuals, contributing to important debates on the issues of the day, needs to be asserted. In other words, the academic community has to demonstrate more intellectual courage if it is to begin to challenge the powerful forces that threaten to undermine the vital function of universities in a democratic society.

30 June 2009

Society 4

The banality of fame

Alex Wood

Last week in Madrid, in the Prado, I discovered Dürer's self-portrait. It shows a young man of 26, face ringed in curling locks, flamboyant, elegant, aristocratic and boldly asserting his artistic status. For all that such a work might be arrogant, this is not. Its inscription, 'I have thus painted myself. I was 26 years old. Albrecht Dürer', is the naïve, almost innocent confidence of youth, the wayward and indomitable bravura of the as-yet unhumbled.

In the Reina Sofia Centre, Picasso's *Guernica* dwarfs its gallery. There is nothing elegant or innocent about *Guernica*, the portrayal of the obliteration of the cultural capital of the Basques by air-borne fascist bombing. Its potent depiction of pain, death and destruction creates a monument to 20th-century man's inhumanity to man.

When he painted *Guernica*, Picasso had experienced a rigorous and classical artistic education, was 55 years old, of plain appearance, married but with a history of many lovers and several mistresses, a man of the world who had seen the canker at the heart of life but remained committed to his art as well as to core values of human decency. *Guernica* was his statement to the world of his 'abhorrence of the military caste which has sunk Spain in an ocean of pain and death'.

During the week that I saw these works, the unfolding news story was of Susan Boyle. She has a powerful and beautiful voice but caution is required about the Damascine conversions of many of those who heard her on *Britain's Got Talent*. The obsession with physical beauty, innate, surgically-created or a result of photographic-editing, remains unchallenged. The red-tops pander to their readers with tasteless speculation about Susan Boyle's private life. To ridicule a performer for her plain looks was seen as banal but the very stuff of such programmes is to ridicule 'losers' and is it not significant that in today's youth culture 'loser' is among the most common of insults?

The Susan Boyle story will be a nine-day wonder. Like the facile anguish at the deaths of Princess Diana and Jade Goody, it permits mass self-delusion. The brief popular identification with the success of 'the ordinary' Susan Boyle cannot detract from the barely concealed relief that her characteristics and life-style are not shared by those who purport to identify with her. Elaine Paige, whom Susan Boyle admires, offers shallow platitudes: 'She is a role model for everyone who has a dream.' To what aspect of Susan Boyle does Paige refer: her superb voice, her long record of family caring or her winning a televised competition?

Similarly, the temporary admiration of her virtues will not lead to growth in the practice of chastity, dedicated caring for parents or devout Catholicism. Although she is now apparently the idol of Blackburn, ridicule, sadly, has been her past portion there as much as on her initial TV appearance.

Susan Boyle deserves to enjoy her success. She should be aware that there will be many who simply admire her voice and how she can use it. Although talented, she is neither youthful nor physically beautiful, as was Dürer. That may be to her advantage. In age and appearance she is closer to the Picasso of the 1930s. Her life experiences are as different from his as could be imagined but they may be sufficiently strong to allow her, with the help and support of genuine friends, to withstand the pressures which will now face her.

More pressing is how our society can withstand the shallow commercialism of a world where instant success, through stage-managed competitions, whether for artists, singers or entrepreneurial apprentices, is perceived as a route to excellence. Neither Dürer nor Picasso could have emerged from such a banal process.

21 April 2009

Part IV

Politics

Politics 1

Eastenders

Kenneth Roy

A young woman pushing a pram tentatively boarded the Easterhouse bus. In her hand was a £20 note. I remembered Mujdeh Yousef, recently arrived from Afghanistan, whose husband also had a £20 note – his only one – and, having inserted it in the cash machine of a Glasgow bus, was told by the driver that it was exact fare only; no change, no charity. The present holder of the £20 note was better informed. She proffered it without hope to the driver, who shook his head. What next....?

The orthodox plot tells us that she should have been thrown off the bus. But she wasn't. Instead she was ushered inside and asked by the driver to trade her £20 note for smaller denominations acceptable to the cash machine. A couple helped out (others, fumbling in their purses, would have done so had they been able) and the woman was almost pathetically grateful, thanking her rescuers three times during the course of her brief journey. I wonder what would have happened if no one on the bus had had change of £20. Actually, I don't wonder: I am fairly sure. The driver would have turned a blind eye, and she would have travelled for free. I know the driver's first name – many addressed him by it – but I will not publish it. He deserves to keep his job.

After she left, I watched her push the pram up a narrow, deserted, tree-lined path to a destination not in view. And I thought: how vulnerable she is making herself; for the second time within minutes, how exposed is her position.

Who designed this path? Who thought it a good idea?

When the bus reached Easterhouse, no great distance from the city centre despite its reputation as a terrifying outer ghetto, I was disappointed not to be confronted by drug-crazed welfare dependents with two heads, living out their sad, crushed existence in streets of boarded-up windows and overgrown gardens pock-marked by infected needles. Really, I was just anxious to confirm the stereotypes and return to civilisation with a routine 'Isn't it awful' story. But the expected copy was already perversely failing to materialise. Instead I found myself mentally noting a shopping centre dominated by the quintessentially suburban 'Next'.

I looked up at the sky. It was big. I looked all around me. It appeared to be safe. The streets were wide and the houses modern, trim, suburban-respectable. One had far too many garden gnomes – as scary in large numbers as drug-crazed welfare dependents with two heads. With my usual facility for failing to spot the story, I had ended up in the wrong Easterhouse. I might as well have gone to Prestwick.

There had not been much sign of political activity earlier in the day. The most numerous street posters belonged to the SNP and Labour – Labour perhaps slightly ahead, these arch enemies often clinging to the same lamp-posts, above or below according to who had got there first – with the Scottish Conservatives and Unionists trailing in third place and the Lib Dems almost invisible. This could be the final result and, if it is, remember you read it here first. Yet in all my many hours trudging round the constituency, I didn't spot a single canvasser.

Here in Easterhouse, however, was a Solidarity stand. I accepted their leaflet and was greeted like a long-lost socialist brother by a gutsy, talkative woman who announced herself as Tommy Sheridan's mum.

Tommy isn't standing this time, except in the dock in due course. He is represented in Glasgow East by Trisha, who has lived in Shettleston for 25 years – I have Mrs Sheridan's word for that. I said to her that Trisha looked young (by which I meant young and attractive) and Mrs Sheridan replied with mock envy that the lovely Trisha had no right to look so young.

'How do you think you're going to do in the by-election?', I asked.

'I think we're going to get a good vote,' she said, which I took to mean that Solidarity stood no chance whatsoever. 'I mean, Labour's been in power for years here and what have they done for Easterhouse? Look at the state of the place.'

I hesitated to mention the profusion of garden gnomes and

the possible implications for the future of the class struggle.

The Easterhouse bus was a wimpish departure from the rule of the day, which was to walk everywhere – from the Radisson Hotel in Argyll Street along the endless Gallowgate in search of deepest Shettleston. At one stage, I asked a friendly native (we were still in the land of one-headed humans) for the whereabouts of Shettleston Road. 'Oh, it's too far to walk,' she advised. 'Take the bus.' 'But I'm in the mood for a long walk,' I said. 'Then carry on till you come to the Forge,' she said. I have forgotten what I was supposed to do when I came to the Forge, but I looked forward to stumbling on this last vestige of the industrial revolution. Sadly, the Forge turned out to be just another retail experience.

I had a pit-stop at the Healthy Eating Centre in Parkhead, not, as it sounds, one of the great oxymorons of our time, but a modern cafe offering life-saving smoothies to bemused journalists. It was so wholesome that it made me long for a seriously squalid little pub, of which there is no shortage in Glasgow East. I found one easily enough – you simply walk 10 yards in any direction – but it was not decadent enough for my taste; it was a cosy snug and unlike most pubs in the district it was unashamedly agnostic.

A smiley middle-aged woman in a red top was chatting up, or being chatted up, by a chap in a smart shirt who uttered the f-word a lot, but relatively inoffensively. Could he be the notorious Shettleston Man who has become such a mascot of this campaign – the ill-educated alcoholic with the bad back, economically inactive, doomed to die at 61? He seemed too rudely chirpy and his woman was intelligent enough for literary allusions. I couldn't decide if they were an official item or afternoon lovers and decided they were the latter. A poor decrepit wee soul wandered in, not long for this world she seemed, and the smiley woman went up to her and hugged her tenderly. A dog of one of the customers was let loose, sniffing discreetly about the place, droopily part of the melancholy, warm, four o'clock, third race of the afternoon mood, as the awful John McCrirrick droned on in the background, unheard, unwatched. I had a pint, my first in a long time, and enjoyed it, and felt relaxed here in the heart of the most deprived place in

Britain, if not Western Europe, if not the civilised world; or whatever. I would not have felt so at home in one of the Rangers pubs, which seemed sullen and withdrawn, while the brighter Celtic pubs, which I might have preferred, were still in mourning for Tommy Burns, who died in early June.

This has been called the 'broken society by-election', a shorthand term cooked up by metropolitan politicians and journalists. The statistics of social disintegration in Glasgow East are indeed appalling, if you believe even half of them. They are so frequently quoted they have become a cliché in themselves; so, forgive me, if you want the latest figures, you must look elsewhere.

A divided, tribal society it certainly is. The divide is not between states of economic well-being – almost everyone is materially poor; nor between races – almost everyone is white (I spotted one black face, a young man emerging from a house in Easterhouse); nor between political philosophies – almost everyone is instinctively of the left. The divide is sectarian, deep, unchanged by time or tide. The boundaries between blue and green are so abrupt that you get quite a shock when you discover you have crossed from one to another. It takes an expert to negotiate that Glasgow minefield.

But a broken society? To have nothing, to have no desire for the conventions of work and mortgage, to be a single parent dependent on the state, to be addicted to alcohol, to fall ill and die young – all this is bad stuff, as we are constantly reminded during this campaign. The mere mention of the constituency and its problems, 'another country' as the Conservative press has stigmatised it, was enough to draw gasps at a recent Westminster drinks party, just before everyone headed off for Cornwall. But anyone who spends any time in the east end of Glasgow will discover that, despite everything, humanity survives; love survives; generosity of spirit survives; caring for each other survives; camaraderie survives; a sense of community survives. This is the inconvenient truth, the paradox at the heart of it all – the east end isn't broken at all.

15 July 2008

Politics 2

Corruptions

Kenneth Roy

Jack McConnell was annoyed – no, angry – actually, hopping mad – over my reference in the weekend edition to 'corruptions' within the Labour administration in Scotland (1999-2007). He took this as an attack on his financial probity and that of his colleagues. It wasn't. It couldn't be: there was nothing to attack. I think, have always thought, of the former First Minister as someone of integrity, able and likeable, and I am sorry for upsetting him. Even if there had been financial corruptions within the Labour administration in Scotland, which there weren't, it is unlikely that I would have written about them. There are invariably more interesting things to write about, particularly with the irrepressible Alex Salmond around.

Is this the end of the matter? Not quite. Jack has said that he would welcome clarification of what I meant by the word 'corruptions'.

To answer this question, I have to go back to the autumn of 2004, when the killing in Iraq was causing distress to many people, particularly those who had in good faith voted Labour for both the Westminster and Holyrood parliaments. On 4 November that year, three Black Watch soldiers from Fife – Sgt Stuart Gray, 31, Pte Paul Lowe, 19, and Pte Scott McArdle, 22 – were part of a deployment supporting American troops in central Iraq. A suicide bomber drove his vehicle at the soldiers, detonating a device and killing all three instantly. They were the first Black Watch casualties in Iraq, as well as the first British victims of suicide attacks.

In that bleak month, with three young Scots dead on the battlefield, support for the war plummeting, politicians held in general contempt, it was business as usual in the various asylums of government and the media. Eight days later, on 12 November, the press-sponsored Scottish politician of the year awards went ahead in Prestonfield House Hotel, Edinburgh.

Among the many politicians present was a leading figure in the Labour establishment, Lord Watson of Invergowrie, an MSP and, until the previous year, a member of the coalition cabinet led by Jack McConnell.

After a disagreement with the staff, Lord Watson set fire to a curtain in the hotel. Although the evidence of his guilt was incontrovertible – he had been caught on CCTV – he protested his innocence. He then changed his plea and was sentenced to 16 months' imprisonment for wilful fire-raising (known in the English jurisdiction as arson) to the endangerment of life. Remarkably, a social enquiry report concluded that he was at significant risk of re-offending.

Not all corruption, then, is financial. Financial corruption in politics is the least of it: no one dies. Setting fire to a hotel curtain, endangering life, when you are an elected servant of the people, a member of the House of Lords, sufficiently highly regarded to have been a senior minister in the early stages of a devolved Scottish government – now, that truly corrupts. It corrupts in the sense that it taints and spoils all you have ever touched. Fortunately, no one died that night. But the timing of the wretched man's irresponsibility could scarcely have been worse, juxtaposed as it was with reports of the return of the soldiers' bodies, the funerals, the anger and grief of the families. Why was Lord Watson of Invergowrie there that night? Why were any of them there? Only connect. Except they so rarely do.

Not all corruption is personal. The worst is state-generated. It is built on deception. A greater concern than the criminal excess of misbehaviour at some awards beanfeast is the question of why Stuart Gray, Paul Lowe and Scott McArdle were in Iraq in the first place. Because Tony loved George? Because George loved Tony? Because Tony loved God? Because God loved Tony? Who knows? Our masters said one thing – the opposite proved to be the case. This time people did die, in their hundreds of thousands. We do not know exactly how many, for nobody was bothering to count.

These corruptions dealt an irreparable blow to the humanitarian ideals and principles on which the Labour party was founded. Should we hold the administration in Scotland blameless? Not in the least. North or south, each appointee of the governing party of the United Kingdom shared some degree of moral responsibility although, of course, the degree differed. Reserved power: I have become quite sick of that term as a way of distancing or absolving the devolved from the iniquities perpetrated by the devolvers. The deplorable treatment of asylum seekers in Glasgow, including the victims of the unjustifiable war in Iraq and the unwinnable one in Afghanistan, the hauling of innocent children from their beds in the early morning, their incarceration for months in detention centres, their ultimate deportation – where is the morality in that? A reserved power, of course. Just like killing people. But conscience is not a reserved power. Humanity is not a reserved power. Who in Scotland resigned? In the face of the killing fields, in the face of the official lies, who sacrificed position and advancement? There are times when business as usual is not business worth conducting.

Time passes. Jack McConnell erroneously claims that I have been consistently critical of his record in office; on the contrary, there was much to admire in his level-headed stewardship. A man of his considerable talents should have been given a peerage and a Westminster ministry; he has been given neither. Lord Watson of Invergowrie, on the other hand, debarred by the length of his sentence from standing for the Scottish parliament again, has been rehabilitated as an active member of the House of Lords and as a public affairs consultant.

In January 2005, two months after his death in Iraq, Scott McArdle's girlfriend gave birth to their child. He and another soldier, Marc Ferns, also a private in the Black Watch, who was killed in Iraq on 12 August 2004, aged 21, are remembered in a memorial of plain dignity in their home town of Glenrothes, Fife, where, four Novembers later, there is soon to be a by-election.

21 October 2008

My prediction of a Labour victory in the Glasgow East by-election proved mistaken: the SNP took the seat. Against most expectations, however, Labour held Glenrothes. – Ed.

Politics 3

Why don't we rock the boat?

Kenneth Roy

Some years ago, a rising star of the Scottish Executive (as it then was) – not one of those here today, gone tomorrow politicians, but someone real and solid, a public official – said to me: 'Of course, we're going to buy you lot off'. I had never been described as part of a lot before. I had spent most of my life trying not to be part of a lot. 'What on earth do you mean?', I replied; or words to that effect.

Well, it was like this. The 'lot' to which he or she referred was the voluntary sector, 'third sector' as it is fashionably known, or more broadly 'civil society', a phrase almost as irritating as 'fit for purpose' but descriptive of the many important people, uniformly fit for purpose, who clog the Glasgow to Edinburgh train with their laptops and graphs and ever-bleeping mobile phones and dense reports with the word 'strategy' in the title, most of them destined for the commitee rooms of Holyrood, or other less illustrious committee rooms, each room identically equipped with a flip chart, pads and biros, and small bottles of Campsie Spring. I observe these busy functionaries with an astonishment bordering on awe. What is it all about? What good does any of it do? Why must society be civil? Why cannot it be uncivil and challenging?

Anyway. This person, the public official, reminded me not only that I was, formally at least, part of that hyperactive class of concerned administrators rattling through Polmont station but someone who could look forward to being bought off by the new political establishment. How so? It appeared that I would be given monetary acknowledgement of my worth – a grant of some kind, an incentive to go on doing whatever it was I was doing, crudely speaking a bit of dosh. I was not to get too excited by the prospect. It wouldn't be much. Heavens, no. The country of which we spoke was still called Scotland. But it would be – well, enough.

'Enough for what?' I persisted.

'Enough to buy your silence, of course,' came the reply.

My silence. It was quite an exciting thought. But there was more. In addition to, or in some cases in place of, a bit of dosh, we, the leaders of civil society, would be flattered by some appointment. I was led to understand that there would be many appointments in the years to come, mostly insignificant if not actually meaningless, but conferring minor prestige and a sense of self-justification, an appointment of which one might reasonably boast, modestly of course, at the many gatherings of civil society.

I then asked what, in exchange for our grant and/or appointment and a Christmas card from the First Minister, we were supposed to be silent about.

The answer did not surprise me. We were to be silent about everything that matters: publicly unquestioning and uncritical; discreet gossip permissible in the approved circles of the knowing; 'access' to ministers an occasional treat; civilised lobbying for our 'client group' (another ghastly confection) perfectly okay – but all of this controlled and unthreatening, all conducted within a safe and closed environment, all of us accepting implicitly the unspoken rules of engagement, or rather non-engagement.

Since that curious conversation, I have had cause to think often, with a mixture of sadness and amusement, how prophetic it has turned out to be. I scan the daily papers for evidence of that lively, sceptical 'civil society' monitoring and exposing the actions, utterances, pomposities and delusions of the political class, but find such independent-minded criticism largely wanting; I await with a decreasing sense of expectation the howls of outrage about transparent injustices; I wonder who speaks for the inarticulate and the marginalised and the 25% of our young people who admit to being long-term depressed.

The alternative narrative, of a sort, provided by the opposition parties is ritualistic and self-serving. The indigenous media (I choose to dismiss the incomers as cynical opportunists) to some extent scrutinise the established order, but are too enfeebled by financial restraints to mount the sustained inquiry required. In short, Scotland has become a strangely acquiescent little place.

Maybe we are too worried about the size of next year's grant (more worrying still, the possibility of no grant) to have the courage to say what needs to be said; timorous beasties, the lot of us. Or maybe, our grant secure for the time being, we are too preoccupied by the minutes of the last meeting and the agenda for the next one to see beyond bureaucratic sterility. And, of course, there is always the faint prospect of that long-delayed meeting with The Salmond Himself: so best not be impolite in advance. All these are reasons in a small, incestuous country not to rock the boat.

My hope for 2009 is for a braver, more outspoken and intellectually healthier Scotland. To that hope I say at once: fat chance.

6 January 2009

Politics 4

Two cheers for Holyrood

Kenneth Roy

This, the 100th edition of the Scottish Review online, coincides with the 10th anniversary of devolution. It was on this Thursday in May 1999 that we went to the polls to elect the first Scottish parliament of the modern era. For the print version of the magazine, I had commissioned several dozen Scots – including people of all political persuasions and none – to keep a diary of the day. The results were a little surprising. The prevailing mood was one of optimism, even among the sceptics; the chilliness of that spring day could not quite dispel the human warmth in the air.

In the evening, I went down to the harbourside at Irvine. People were talking animatedly of having voted or of preparing to vote. For once, politics seemed to be generating interest for the right reasons: the sense of history being made was almost palpable. It is true that the mood in the UK as a whole was positive, almost sunny. We were approaching the year 2000 slightly fearful of the bug (as we are now slightly fearful of another bug) but otherwise reasonably content and prosperous. Tony Blair's exceptional political nous had not deserted him. Saddam Hussein clung to power. The twin towers were admired as peaks of American achievement. We thought of banks as citadels of integrity. The house market was buoyant. Diana, Princess of Wales, had acquired a new boyfriend. We hadn't a clue in May 1999 how quickly and completely the world was about to change. We should have made the best of the good times. Maybe to some extent we did.

In Scotland, there were few unrealistic expectations of the new parliament, but a widely held view that it was high time we had one. The compromise – devolution stopping well short of outright independence – suited the cautious character of the Scots, while the man in charge, Donald Dewar, commanded general respect for his good mind and seriousness of purpose.

Later in the year, he justified the existence of the parliament with a piece of superb oratory. His early death was wretched misfortune, taking some of the fizz out of the new deal. But the coalition administration pointed to a new, less adversarial form of politics, just as the subsequent minority government has proved to be workable. These Scottish experiments, confounding tired Westminster orthodoxy, have been far from failures.

It would not be difficult to pick holes in the record of the first 10 years. The system of election, combining first past the post with a party list, is profoundly undemocratic and ought to be reformed. The right of members to sit in both the Scottish and UK parliaments should never have been allowed. Furthermore, it is bizarre that Lord Foulkes (the disgraced Lord Watson before him) has a berth at Holyrood and in the House of Lords. If MSPs wish to be taken seriously, they should be full-time and not also be engaged in the Lords, the Court of Session or elsewhere. There are few of outstanding personality and the original vision of encouraging into politics people of all the talents has never been remotely fulfilled. The standard of debating is abysmal. The hideously expensive parliament building, which feels crushed for space at the foot of the royal mile, is an obvious candidate for demolition long before the century expires. The present First Minister, though capable, is somehow annoying, sharing some of Mr Blair's liking for the company of celebrities. These are among the more obvious downsides. They are considerable.

The devolved parliament has been kind to old people, students, people on prescription drugs and motorists who require to cross bridges. These easy hits have invited accusations of populism. The health of the nation remains woefully poor, the life expectancy of Shettleston Man having improved not a jot in 10 years, and education is as big a mess as ever. What, ask the parliament's many critics, has devolution done for Scotland? In practical terms it has been doodling on the margins. But I wonder if anyone genuinely believed in May 1999 that it would initially do much more.

Its main achievement seems to me to be one of perception and atmosphere rather than of tangible improvement. For all its many failings, the Holyrood set-up now looks more credible than Westminster. It is less confrontational. There is greater transparency, over expenses and more generally. Politically, the Scottish administrations have steered a moderate, left-of-centre course; had it been down to Holyrood there would, for example, have been no ID card scheme. The present ministerial team, whatever one thinks of their party's long-term goal, is fairly bright and humane. The corrosive public disenchantment with politics, the collapse of faith in political institutions, is largely a UK phenomenon; I do not detect that it has infected Scotland to the same extent. There is still some hope left; still a willingness to give the parliament the benefit of the doubt. So the last 10 years are worth, if not a resounding three cheers, a tentative two.

7 May 2009

You may have spotted a factual error in this piece. If you have not spotted it, you may wish to turn to the final article in this volume, where the error will be revealed. On the other hand, you may wish to restrain your curiosity and go on reading the book in its order of contents. – Ed.

Part V

Obama

Obama 1

Praying for the president

R D Kernohan's election night diary

10.00pm
I am filling in some of the waiting time reading about the life of Wallenstein by Golo Mann (son of Thomas). It is a reminder of the way that so many dazzling triumphs set in train events that end in tears.

11.30pm
Even with polls still open and no proper results, I am already tiring of commentators warming up with talk of a 'historic vote for change' and the 'first black president' (for some of them have temporarily set aside the politically correct 'African American'). Of course they are bound to, for facts are chiels that winna ding. But two points can be missed.

Any good Democrat ought to win this election, even without the financial crisis and looming recession, for the Bush administration never recovered from the mishandled aftermath of the Iraq war and defeat in the mid-term Congressional elections. And Obama's successes, against Hillary and in dominating the campaign with McCain trying to catch up, were possible because black America had already broken the barriers. Colin Powell, Condoleezza Rice, even Tiger Woods, made it possible for Obama to aim for the top.

1.00am
As early results trickle in I switch channels and also try the internet. The BBC seems not bad but the best bet is CNN, although the sheer complexity of its coverage of Congressional and gubernatorial elections makes it hard to take in everything. But Americans seem reluctant to emphasise local swings from 2004 and very cautious about exit polls, perhaps because they've burned some fingers in the past. However as I write there's an analysis of Indiana counties which suggests a marked swing to

Obama from Kerry's showing last time. Then comes something similar in Virginia and Florida.

2.00am

And so to prayer. My evening prayers have been understandably delayed. But my prayers for the next president of the USA have to be in two kinds, one of which sets my instinct at odds with my intellect. I have no problem praying that he will be sustained and well guided, for I have experienced once or twice an extraordinary sense of being supported by the prayers of other people, known and unknown to me. But my instinct is also to pray that he be preserved from harm and spared from the murderous fanaticism which killed Lincoln and Kennedy (inter alia) and nearly killed Reagan. That instinct is more powerful than my doubts, but my reason tells me that God, who devolved such power to humanity and offered it a pattern, is now disinclined to supernatural intervention with the course of nature and consequences of free will. Maybe I should also be praying for the mentally unstable and for the bodyguards.

7.00am

Got up to check the result and heard replay of Obama's victory speech. As such things go it was pretty good – Lincoln from Illinois, the American Dream, and echoes of Martin Luther King. The energy and the eloquence are real but I worry about the weight of expectations that now fall on him. A lot of people are going to be disappointed – if not soon, certainly later.

7.24am

Stayed with Radio Scotland to see how their *Thought for the Day* coped, given the BBC's passion in recent times for scripts to be cleared well in advance and stuck to. It was fine, but if I had been doing it I'd have wanted two scripts cleared: one that was cautious and hedged about enough to let Obama's name be put in or taken out as necessary and one that from the start assumed he would win and looked at that undue weight of expectation and at the consequences of overwhelming black support and very marked white hesitation. And I would have prayed again for him, as I do.

10.00am

McCain emerged with honour. His one real mistake was Sarah Palin, who from the start was exposed to ruthless, predictable assault and battery from the all-too-liberal media. Maybe the Republicans should have saved her for consideration in 2012. Their poor showing in the Congressional elections will add to their difficulties ahead. They will want a new prophet (or better still, a prophetess) but conditions will make it hard for one to emerge. The Mormon Mitt Romney at 61 might still have a future but he's no more an Obama than he is a Brigham Young. I suppose there will be chatter about the Austro-Californian bodybuilder but he's still rightly ruled out.

10.30am

There's too long to wait for the inauguration, though before Roosevelt's time it was even longer. A constitutional change by agreement might be appropriate for future elections.

5 November 2008

Obama 2

My friend Barack

Kenneth Roy

Britain may be facing the worst recession in Europe, with the possible exception of Latvia, but the habits of dress-down Friday die hard. It is impossible to do business beyond lunchtime and by the middle of the afternoon the mighty fax is silent, the phone never rings and the e-mail has ceased to ping; around 4, our neighbours in the building start drifting off for an unhappy weekend of worrying about Christmas. Last Friday, however, was different. At 5.40, I was slumped at my desk in the usual fashion when, lo and behold, the e-mail did ping – a strange sound in the pervasive silence of 66 John Finnie Street – and I found myself muttering aloud: 'Who on earth can that be, this late on a Friday night?'

Of course: I should have guessed. It was Barack.

'Kenneth –,' he began in his characteristically direct manner. He just wanted to let me know how the week had gone: nothing too drastic; all more or less according to plan; and wondering if I'd be able to join him in Grant Park for the election night party. True to form, he ended by asking me for five dollars. He's a bit like that, Barack – quite upfront about money matters; all part of his irresistible charm. As a foreigner, I am unable to help financially – he should know that by now. But I can still lend a bit of moral support, spreading the word to the lazy Brits who work here in John Finnie Street, or writing relatively nice things about him in the Scottish Review. Even when I write relatively nasty things, he doesn't seem to mind.

For the last 11 months, Barack has been my most frequent and faithful e-mail correspondent. Scarcely a week has gone by without a friendly electronic missive. When he's been away, or exceptionally busy, I invariably hear from one of the team – David, his inexhaustible campaign manager, or Joe Biden (remember him? perhaps not), or the lovely Michelle.

How did this beautiful friendship come about? Like a lot of

people, I was curious about the man who was then a virtually unknown outsider for the Democratic nomination and anxious to know what he stood for, so I logged on to the Barack Obama website and clicked a few boxes. I was still finding it difficult to discover what he stood for, so I clicked a few more boxes, adding my e-mail address. An odd thing then happened: a notice came up thanking me for my interest and enrolling me as one of his supporters. Like so many things in life, it was all just a happy accident.

I have been with Barack ever since. It feels almost like man and boy. To be perfectly frank, I still don't have a clue what he stands for – though he does bang on about the need for change and, depending on the nature of the change, I'm with him there, theoretically. But if I haven't learned much about Barack Obama's policies, I have learned a lot about the most brilliant campaign in electoral history – a campaign whose success owes so much to its exploitation of the internet.

It is often pointed out that Obama has succeeded in raising unthinkable amounts of money from modest donations on the web. This is true, although it is only part of the story. Most of his e-mails have ended with an invitation to hit the 'Donate' box and the amount requested is almost absurdly small – rarely more than 10 dollars – just about enough to finance the downpayment on a glass of dry white wine in your average British four-star hotel. What is less often pointed out is that the accumulation of requests for absurdly small donations adds up, over the course of a year, to a tidy sum.

But even that is only part of the story. The genius of the marketing lies in the perfection of the pitch – informal without being irritating; personal without being ingratiating; serious without being hectoring; graceful under the severest pressure. It is amusing to hear that the political parties in Britain are hoping to learn from the supreme professionalism of these techniques. Dream on, chaps. At the heart of the Obama campaign was the seductive appeal of the candidate himself. We may now have to ditch the once reliable adage that politics is showbiz for ugly people; whatever Obama is (and I'm still far from sure), ugly he ain't. Our lot? Hug-a-hoodie Dave and non-flash Gordon just don't have what it takes to fight an effective internet campaign.

When Vince Cable is the most admired man in British politics, you know you have a charisma problem.

I left the house this morning thinking: well, Barack has got what he wanted; the great prize is his; I suppose the last person he'll be thinking about at the moment is me.

How wrong could I be?

At 5.58am the first e-mail of the day arrived:

Kenneth --

I'm about to head to Grant Park to talk to everyone gathered there, but I wanted to write to you first.

We just made history.

And I don't want you to forget how we did it.

You made history every single day during this campaign – every day you knocked on doors, made a donation, or talked to your family, friends and neighbors about why you believe it's time for change.

I want to thank all of you who gave your time, talent and passion to this campaign.

We have a lot of work to do to get our country back on track, and I'll be in touch soon about what comes next.

But I want to be very clear about one thing...

All of this happened because of you.

Thank you,

Barack

Now, that's what I call customer care.

5 November 2008

Obama 3

The new America

Alan McIntyre

I sat at home in Connecticut last Tuesday night, parked on the sofa from 6pm till 2am with only the occasional trip to the kitchen for beer and snacks. As my wife Maria and I watched the electoral college votes accumulate for Obama we weren't crying with joy or high fiving each other. When the TV networks called it for Obama at 11pm we didn't embrace or go out and party in the streets; but we did smile, relieved that the America we know and love was reasserting itself. Hope and change became clichés in this campaign, repeated ad nauseam by candidates of every persuasion. Nevertheless, watching a dignified and almost sombre Obama take the stage as president-elect there was a sense that this could well be a pivotal moment; maybe Obama could match up to the last skinny guy from Illinois who became president – a certain Abraham Lincoln.

To be clear, we didn't have a horse in this race, or at least not directly. As mere green card holders we are voyeurs of American democracy, subject to taxation without representation as the colonists once complained. But America is our adopted home and we care deeply about the type of society we raise our kids in. Since we moved here in 2005 we've often had to justify our choice to friends and family in Europe, many of whom view our suburban American life as a deprivation to be endured rather than something to be envied.

At its core what attracts us to America, and the reason that we chose to live here, is a variation on the Obama mantra of 'yes we can'. The oft-invoked imagery of America as 'the city on the hill', 'the last best hope for democracy' and often simply as 'the greatest nation on earth' can seem presumptuous and incredibly insular when viewed from across the Atlantic. This combination of patriotism and exceptionalism (often with a dose of divine mission thrown in) has been amplified in the echo chamber of the presidential campaign, but it's also there in our everyday life in the Connecticut suburbs. From the 'Support our Troops' bumper stickers to the ubiquitous singing of the Star Spangled Banner at every public event, there is a passion for this country that you rarely see in Europe outside football stadiums.

But beneath the jingoism and hoopla is something very seductive and attractive; at least for us. At an individual level it's a fundamental optimism that you can create a better life for yourself and your family and that better times lie ahead. It's the community spirit that had our neighbours organise a home-cooked dinner to be delivered to our door at 5pm every night for two weeks when our fourth child was in hospital with meningitis. It's the generosity of spirit that had complete strangers pay our bill at a local restaurant simply because they overheard that we had just moved to America and they wanted to welcome us. While the 'yes we can' attitude is most visible at the local level, it's also occasionally there at the national level in the America of the Marshall Plan and the Peace Corp. That America - while maybe not our last best hope - is certainly a force for good in the world.

Over the last few years it has been hard to hold onto my favourite image of America as a big friendly puppy, wagging its tail in a small room and occasionally knocking over the good ornaments; fundamentally well intentioned but often a bit clumsy in its dealings with the rest of the world. As Churchill famously said, 'Americans can always be counted upon to do the right thing...but only after they have exhausted all the alternatives.' Over the last eight years the Bush administration has appeared to be systematically working its way through that list of alternatives with no 'right thing' in sight. While many of the mistakes can be traced back to the provocation of 9/11, the America of Guantanamo Bay and of Abu Ghraib is not an attractive place. Domestically the drift towards theocracy has also been discouraging. From the hypocrisy of pro-life capital punishment supporters to the continued battle in some school districts to teach Darwinian evolution as more than just a hypothesis, the trend has been negative.

So is the result on Tuesday night a cause for real hope? In his acceptance speech Obama used the life of Ann Nixon Cooper (a 106-year-old black voter from Georgia) to illustrate the dramatic changes in American society over the last century. He could also have used the example of Amanda Jones, a 109-year-old black voter from Texas whose father was actually emancipated from slavery in 1865 at the age of 12. Racial change in America has never come without a struggle. From the horror of 600,000 dead in the Civil War through the civil rights era of the 1960s to the race riots in LA as recently as 1992, America has always struggled with the idea of black equality. In that context, for America to freely elect a black president and for him to win 'white' states such as Iowa and Wisconsin is a true milestone.

An Obama presidency will undoubtedly change how America views itself. A poll taken immediately after the election showed that over two thirds of Americans were both proud and excited to have elected a black president; a result which clearly challenges both the traditional 50/50 politics and the redneck caricature of this country. However, more importantly, Obama's election may help open a new chapter in how America is viewed by the rest of the world and provide an opportunity to reposition this country as a force for good.

Under an Obama administration I will almost certainly pay higher taxes and I may object to a fair swathe of his legislative agenda (although for someone raised in Scotland in the 1970s it seems a long way from socialism as I know it). Nevertheless, if I'd had a vote on Tuesday I would have cast it for Obama. I would have cast it in the hope that he can begin to harness and channel all that is good and admirable in American society and once again make me proud to be at least a temporary American.

11 November 2008

Obama 4

A pragmatic idealist

Andrew Hook

Despite the best efforts of TV reporters, newspaper correspondents, leader-writers and commentators of every kind, I feel that those of us on this side of the Atlantic still do not adequately grasp the full momentousness of Obama's victory for so many millions of Americans. And by this I do not only mean the fact – hugely significant as it is – that a man of mixed race will occupy the White House. What I do mean is that for countless Americans a dark cloud that for eight long years has hung depressingly over their country has at last been dispelled.

Don't take my word for it. Listen to the spontaneous voices of Americans themselves. Here is Nell, from Charlottesville, Virginia, currently a postgraduate student in Columbia University in New York: 'O Andrew! I've been running around being totally distracted and now elated about it all! I am so proud of Virginia! So proud of everyone! It's just such a wonderful moment. I really do feel like it's just a moment of catharsis. We really have something to be proud of again and it just feels so good. So so good. I can't describe it all. The feeling here is incredible. People are just so happy. It feels like everyone has such good will towards everyone else. There is so much happiness. I can't stop looking at all the photographs and listening to the news and crying! It's wonderful. Just wonderful.'

Jennifer, on the other hand, is a junior academic, with a tenure-track position teaching Russian studies at Bard College in upper state New York: 'My dear Andrew – I just have to write you and express how happy and exhilarated we all are! It's an incredible feeling to be newly inspired and newly hopeful in my fellow Americans and in all this means for the state of the world. It's hard to overstate how built-up so many important questions have become, how much emotional and psychological baggage has accumulated in the last eight years, and how lightened I (we) feel today.'

Finally, here is Daniel, a senior professor in the English department at Central Michigan University: 'Greetings, Andrew. That was a very emotional night. About a week before election day I granted myself permission to begin to believe that Obama would win, as all the polls were suggesting. But we've been disappointed before. Terribly disappointed. But this time was different. I feel as if I have my country back. I actually feel pride in what we have done. I won't go on and on about this, but I believe that this is a truly historic renewal of hope that at least some of the vaunted ideals might find some traction in the world.'

Okay, all three voices emerge out of educated, academic backgrounds. But they are no less representative for that. (Remember that in the election more graduates voted Democratic than non-graduates.) And surely the sentiments of my three friends are exactly what we saw in the faces of the many thousands of Americans who filled Grant Park in Chicago last Tuesday night listening to Barack Obama's victory speech.

Will the new president be able to fulfil the lofty expectations he has created? My own view is that he will prove a pretty pragmatic idealist. Like so many others, I hope that immediately after his inauguration there will be some dramatic, symbolic gestures: the closing down of Guantanamo Bay, the ending of torture, the restoration of prisoners' rights, perhaps the legalising of stem-cell research. But on the big issues of the economy and foreign policy, pragmatism will prevail – even if perhaps with a more human face.

Fortunately, in terms of getting things done, President Obama will enjoy the most favourable of winds. In the House of Representatives the Democrats will enjoy an increased, very substantial majority. In the Senate they will fall short of the magical, filibuster-proof, 60 seats – but by the narrowest of margins. In any event, it is highly unlikely that the Republican minority in the Senate will try seriously to disrupt or delay the Democratic legislative programme. Nineteen Republican senators are up for re-election in 2010. Few of them will be willing to be seen as responsible for trying to frustrate new Democratic policies legitimised by such large majorities both inside and outside Congress. On the economy in particular there will be enormous pressure on the Republicans to work with the Demcrats to find solutions to the current crisis.

In fact, as a result of this election defeat, it is the Republican party that finds itself facing enormous problems. Admittedly last Tuesday white America voted Republican by a 55-43 margin. Unsurprisingly evangelical Christians also maintained their Republican support 74-24. But much of the statistical polling evidence points in the other direction. The 18-29 age group voted Democratic 66-32. African-Americans inevitably voted overwhelmingly for Obama, but more significantly, Hispanics, the fastest growing minority in the US, voted Democratic 66-32. What does this barrage of statistics mean? The answer is, in the words of a Republican commentator, that 'the Republican base is fast becoming a racial and cultural minority'.

My view is that the fate of Sarah Palin will be the litmus test for the future of the Republican party. If those who are already promoting her as their presidential candidate next time round prevail, then the Democrats will remain in power for a very long time indeed. If on the other hand the woman who apparently thought that Africa was a single country disappears back to Alaska, then the Republican party will be able to begin building a new, broader coalition of voters rejecting the idea, in the words of another commentator, that 'know-nothingness was no longer a stigma, but a badge of honor'.

11 November 2008

Part VI

Small world

Small world 1

Farewell to Serbia

Alan Fisher

On the edge of the Serbian capital lies a suburb known as New Belgrade. It's an area of new apartment blocks and of the biggest shopping mall in the Balkans. It's also the place a man called Dragan Dabic called home. The genial doctor of alternative medicine was a regular at The Crazy House, a small bar on a corner of one of the poorer parts of this sprawling estate. Quietly he would talk about music and books, sipping on his red wine or coffee. He was well liked by the other regulars. No one knew that the man sitting there beside them was the world's most wanted war criminal, Radovan Karadzic.

Last Thursday, they set chairs outside The Crazy House to observe the events in The Hague. The crowd watched intently as Dragan Dabic stood in court accused of mass murder and atrocity. For them, the man on the screen was a stranger – yet someone they all recognised. Above the TV, a portrait – still wet – of a face they knew better.

Tomas Kovijanic, the bar owner, often served Dragan Dabic. Watching the man he's proud to call a friend appear in the dock, he told me: 'Like every true Serb patriot, I am sad and unhappy. Radovan is not with us now and he is in a place he does not deserve to be. But I am proud because in my bar he spent the last couple of years enjoying freedom while the whole world was searching for him.'

One man seemed to be following events more closely than the others. He confided in me that he had been a Serb soldier. Shaking with anger, close to tears, he said he witnessed many horrors during the war in the early nineties. 'I saw the massacre of Serbs, many bodies of dead children. It is unjust to accuse one side all the time and not do anything about the other.'

Across Serbia there are still sharp divisions about what has happened to Radovan Karadzic – those who believe he should face the court, others like those in The Crazy House who regard him as a Serb hero. But for one man it's personal – Luka Karadzic.

In the days following the arrest, Luka rarely spoke at length to the media, preferring to pass just a few comments outside the court in Belgrade where his brother was being held. But at the edge of one protest, he stopped to speak to me. Everyone wanted to know how Karadzic had managed to evade the authorities for so long. Luka suggested that it took more than a good disguise for his brother to remain free. 'He is a smart and skilful man. He knows the spirit of the people. I don't know how he fell after so many years. It was probably an act of treason. What happened is still unclear to me and to him.'

The brothers have discussed the charges Karadzic faces. Luka believes the court will see that it has no basis to proceed. 'I don't think anything positive about the tribunal. All the worst things that could be put into the indictment have been put there, but there is no link to my brother. People who know him, they know that Radovan is not a murderer. He is a doctor, a humanist, a poet, an intellectual, a man who helped many Muslims and Croats and Serbs. And even in his second identity as Dr Dabic he treated members of every nationality.'

Luka plans to continue his daily protests. But he accepts that while he is on the streets of Belgrade, his brother will be thousands of miles away, in a cell in The Hague.

5 August 2008

Small world 2

Arrested in Israel

Alan Fisher

Thursday 1 January

A new year, but the conflict which has dominated world events for the past 60 years goes on with the same intensity and bitterness. It's a bad start to the day when our attempts to film Israeli tanks close to the Erez border crossing are blocked again by Israeli police. They are polite but insistent – this is a closed military area and we have to go.

So we head to a point on the main road, close to a place signposted Armistice House. This was a place used for meetings between Israelis and Egyptians to discuss a ceasefire after the war in 1948. Here we can see Gaza in the distance. And throughout the day explosions cut through the air and huge plumes of smoke follow.

At one point a grey streak of smoke shoots upwards – a missile fired out of Gaza, heading towards Be'er Sheva. Within two minutes, from the spot where the trail appeared to start, there's an explosion and a huge ball of smoke as the Israelis strike back immediately.

Throughout the afternoon, there is a series of loud explosions after a number of attacks from the air. It's thought that the Israelis are targeting the minefields and booby traps laid by the Palestinians, literally preparing the ground for a land offensive. It's a big gamble and the international community has a very small window to forge a deal which will stop it happening.

Friday 2 January

Just before 8am the sirens suddenly sound at our hotel in Ashkelon. Two loud droning noises followed by a voice in Hebrew then in English – 'Will all guests please make their way to a secure place'. Rockets from Gaza are on their way. Within seconds there are two loud explosions. Ashkelon is the target. I'm told seven have landed in the city. There is some damage to one house and minor scratches to one resident. It's a reminder of how notoriously inaccurate these rockets are, and how they are indiscriminate in their targeting.

As a matter of curiosity I go to check out the secure room on my floor. It is essentially a windowless conference room with chairs arranged around makeshift tables and a steel ladder which leads to the floor above. It provides more than adequate protection because the chances of a direct strike are so small.

Kissafim is a border crossing between Israel and Gaza. It's deserted. As we drive towards it, it's eerie just how quiet it is. As I stand looking into Gaza, the silence is broken by the call to Friday prayer carried in the wind. It's suddenly drowned out by three loud explosions to my right, somewhere in the distance. As I try to find out what has been hit, another three echo around the area. Suddenly the drone of aircraft is also noticeable as Israeli spotter aircraft do their job in the skies above me. I walk past the yellow permanent roadblocks and make my way to the border. It's marked by a fence which is possibly electrified and heavy concrete blocks. This is the very edge of Israel.

Our presence is suddenly the subject of attention from the Israeli army. Three vehicles surround us and ask what we're doing. We explain and they insist we hand over the tapes. Our local producer, Yossi, tries to tell them we have nothing that shows the army, but we're reminded that we are filming in a closed military zone and co-operation is not optional. They take our camera.

I'm writing this in the back of our car. We've asked the soliders to refer the matter higher, and they've agreed. I suspect we've lost our morning's work. Our encounter on the border is perhaps an example of how edgy everyone is. If a ground assault is to go ahead, and all the signs are that it is, it's going to happen in the next 48 to 72 hours.

Later that day
We're detained by the Israeli army while filming close to the border with Gaza. They tell us that we are in a closed military area despite having passed two police patrols on the way there. The army holds us for four hours before passing us into police custody. Our vehicle is ordered to follow the police to the base at

Ofa Kim. I'm taken into a small room where I'm questioned by a detective, who shows me a notice in Hebrew which he says is an order stopping unauthorised people entering the area where we were detained. I point out I don't read Hebrew. He then asks several questions which results in the same answer: 'I don't read Hebrew'.

I have discovered that another news team had been in the area yesterday and I point this out. I tell the police that they aired footage from the so-called closed area and wonder why it is just an Al Jazeera team which has run into problems when there are hundreds of journalists doing what we've just done. The bespectled shaven-haired officer has the decency to look slightly uncomfortable before insisting our detention is nothing to do with who we work for. My cameraman is offered coffee. I'm asked if I want anything and request 'our tapes and to leave'. There is no smile. I'm told that we can't leave. We have to be 'processed' which sounds ominous.

After two hours with the police an army team show up to view the material we have filmed. They tell us that we can't have the discs back as they show something that is restricted. I ask what, and the young male officer is about to answer when he realises what he's about to do and says he can't say. Almost.

I'm then asked to sign a statement in Hebrew which will release me on bail. I tell the clerk that I don't read Hebrew so our producer is called who checks over the wording and nods. I'm agreeing to stay out of the closed military zone. I sign to end this seven-hour drag of pain and inconvenience. The soldiers and police have been professional rather than friendly, but we've lost a whole day.

My producer smiles at me as we get into the car. 'They are embarrassed. We should never have gotten so far.' It doesn't make me feel any better.

6 January 2009

Small world 3

Copenhagen ghost

Alan Fisher

We meet near a railway station close to the centre of Copenhagen. He has thick black hair swept back and a jacket that looks too thin in the biting cold of the late afternoon. Ahmed, it's not his real name, has been in Denmark for a long time – he doesn't want to say how long. He came from Turkey. His father was a member of the PKK, a group fighting to create a Kurdish homeland. But he was killed by Turkish army special forces. Ahmed was then served his conscription papers for the Turkish army, but he didn't want anything to do with the people who killed his father. He was worried he too would be killed. So he ran. First to Germany, then on to Denmark.

He applied for asylum and waited three years for a decision. His lawyer argued that his life was at risk and that because of his family connections he simply couldn't return. The Danish panel listened carefully, and then ruled against him. At the asylum centre, he waited and wondered when they would come to deport him. At that point Ahmed decided he couldn't let that happen, and so he disappeared. He walked out of the camp and became a ghost.

He lives in an apartment, he works sometimes, he even has a family but to the Danish authorities he doesn't exist.

'I cannot get sick. If I went to a doctor or a hospital, that would let people know where I am. I rarely go out. Even being here with you is a risk. I try to be invisible.'

He helps with the cost of running his home by taking odd jobs for cash where he can. In his faltering English he tells me: 'I know the pay is poor. I know it's much less than they would pay normally but what else can I do? I cannot complain. I need the money.'

As we walk by the river we talk about the life he left behind. 'I love my land. I love the people there, my family. I have not spoken to them for years. I cannot come to the surface.' I ask what the hardest thing is about staying hidden. His head drops and he speaks slowly and quietly: 'I have to lie, it seems all the time. And I have to remember what lies I have told. What names, what stories, what places. It is very stressful but I do not like to lie. Every day I worry I will slip up on one little thing and that will be enough. They will come, there will be a knock on the door and I will be taken away.'

Michala Clante Bendixen helps run the underground committee for refugees in Copenhagen. A graphic artist, she does what she can to help those who have lost their cases and melted away to join the faces in the crowd. 'There are many like Ahmed. If he returns, he could be killed because of his family connections. Under EU rules, he could apply for asylum again because his country is considered dangerous but if he filed papers, they would know where he was and deport him before the case could be heard. He cannot win so has to live the way he does.'

Ahmed says that maybe one day it will be safe for him to return to his homeland but for the moment Denmark is where he lives – in full sight, but invisible.

17 March 2009

Small world 4

Death of a patriarch

Alan Fisher

5 December

Russia's 'Pope' has died. The patriarch of the Russian Orthodox Church was a significant figure around the country.

Alexiy II was the first leader of the church who was elected without government interference. That was in 1990, in the dying days of communism in this country. And as a new state emerged, he returned the orthodoxy to a prominent role, oversaw the restoration of buidlings that had been abandoned or converted and encouraged a surge in faith which brought hundreds of thousands back to the church.

As the news breaks we head to the site of Moscow's huge and impressive cathedral. It's obvious many people here have not heard. When we look for a reaction, one woman asks 'Is it true?'. When we tell her it is, she blinks, shivers and replies: 'He was a saint. Every day I pass by here and pray.' She turns to the cathedral and crosses herself several times, ferociously swallowing back the tears.

Alexiy was an interesting character. Born in Estonia, he decided to take up a life in religion at the time it was surpressed by the communist authorities. He quickly rose though the heirarchy: bishop at 32, archbishop at 35. And eventually he made his way to the church's headquarters in Moscow.

For years he was accused of being an agent for the notorious secret police, the KGB – his name was found in files when communism collapsed. The church always denied the claims. Alexiy insisted compromises had to be made to allow people to continue to worship, to allow priests to avoid persecution. And no more was said.

The Russian Orthodox Church is the third biggest Christian community in the world. Its power base is in Russia where most of its 135 million adherents live, but it has branches in China, Japan, the USA, across Europe – in fact, wherever Russians have settled.

He grew close to the Kremlin, often aligning the church with its foreign policy and that's reflected in the warm tributes from president and prime minister. His funeral on Tuesday will be a solemn celebration of the man who took over a church that officially didn't exist in agnostic, communist Russia and made it a significant power in the land.

7 December
Moscow is enjoying unseasonably warm weather. Normally at this time of year snow blankets the ground and temperatures rarely climb above freezing. It's warmer here than in Scotland. And that's a little consolation to the tens of thousands of people queuing to pay their last respects to the Russian church's patriarch.

They are waiting for up to five hours to file slowly past the body, which is now lying in Christ the Saviour Cathedral. One woman called Irina tells me she had to travel on three buses to get here. 'I had to say goodbye. My efforts mean little compared to what he did for the church.' People nod in agreement. Police line the route, roads have been closed. It's an impressive display of faith.

9 December 2008

Part VII

Birthdays

Birthdays 1

We like to think he's one of us

Kenneth Roy

After several years of attending and addressing Burns Suppers in Ayrshire, the myth underpinning these annual rituals slowly occurred to me.

The myth could be partially obscured by erudition. One year at the Alloway Burns supper, in a village hall a few yards from the birthplace, my fellow speakers were the Kilmarnock dominie and Labour politician Willie Ross, variously known as the Hammer of the Nats and Old Basso Profundo, and the bow-tied poet and broadcaster Maurice Lindsay. Boy, did they know their stuff. I felt like an imposter.

The myth could be partially obscured by whisky. I drank rather a lot of it then. In the village of Barr, I delivered the toast to the Immortal Memory and sat back well satisfied, determined to enjoy the rest of the night. A few hours later, the chairman whispered in my ear. 'You do know,' he said, 'it's a tradition here that the main speaker proposes another toast at the end?' I did not. I was driven home in time for breakfast by one of the local double-s Fergussons; perhaps the one who is now the presiding officer of the Scottish parliament, perhaps not. Anyway, he had a beard. I remember the beard.

The myth could be partially obscured by character. I surveyed the massed ranks of the male population of the village of Dailly; there could have been few absent. I neither enjoy nor approve of all-male gatherings, but this was an exception. As I delivered the speech – yet another Immortal Memory – I suddenly felt moved, almost to tears, by the rapt attention of these men with their Ayrshire faces, in their formal, old-fashioned suits. It seemed that they had stepped from the pages of Robert Burns's collected works. I sensed strongly for the first time that, in this workaday village, I had reached the heart of Scotland. It is not an emotion I have experienced since, but it was deeply affecting for the hour or so it lasted.

Yet, although it could be partially obscured in these or other ways, there was no denying the existence of the myth or its hold on the national consciousness. In our collective imagination Robert Burns has ceased to be what he was and has been transformed into a caricature. It is significant that at the average Burns supper, the most anticipated turn, the highlight of the occasion, is the toast to The Lassies, a knockabout affair often entrusted to some coarse local comic. It is during this speech that the caricature emerges in all its disfiguring horror: 'Rabbie' (never Robert) as the typical Ayr United supporter, constantly on the pull (wink-wink), knocking it back big time after the gemme (nudge-nudge), generally A Bit Of A Lad. Suddenly, once a year, there is somewhere to put all that national guilt about sex, faithlessness and booze; someone to hang it on; a forgiving recipient of all our excuses. 'Rabbie' is worth celebrating because 'Rabbie' eases the pain.

But that is the least of the myth. We then go further and try to pretend, because it suits our shallow vanity to do so, that Robert Burns was – is – one of us. He isn't. To understand why, we need to de-construct the reputation of Burns as an ill-educated peasant; and then we need to take a hard look at ourselves.

Though it suits our purposes to imagine otherwise, Burns was brought up in a family environment of culture and learning. His father, William, highly intelligent, well-read, deeply serious, would have loathed the typical Burns supper, repelled as he was by all forms of ribaldry; nor was he an admirer of the Scots vernacular, insisting that English be spoken in the home.

He was so concerned for his sons' education that he removed them from the village school, whose standards he considered lax, and set up a small independent school for Robert, his brother Gilbert and a few others, hiring an idealistic teacher, John Murdoch, then still in his teens. Murdoch, despite his youth, was no pushover; his regime was disciplinarian, his curriculum demanding. At the age of six, Robert Burns was 'substituting synonyms', 'supplying ellipses', turning verse into prose, paraphrasing, and learning passages from Shakespeare by heart. When he failed to sing the psalms to Murdoch's satisfaction, he was thrashed with the tawse.

Out of school, Robert and his brother were given books for

their further enlightenment. They included – it is worth naming them, if only in the cause of destroying the myth:

Salmon's *Geographical Grammar*
Dorham's *Physico- and Astro-Theology*
Hervey's *Meditations among the Tombs*
Ray's *Wisdom of God and the Creation*
Taylor's *On Original Sin*

At night, Robert's father took from the shelf a book of geography, theology or natural history for the instruction of his children. As Catherine Carswell wrote in her definitive biography of Burns: 'To him [Robert], the nature of a book had been made so very sacred that to the end of his life he could never surely discriminate between a good book and a bad one.'

By the age of 14 he was teaching himself the rudiments of Latin, though it bored him. France excited him a great deal more.

This, then, was the early life of Robert Burns. What of ourselves – the Burns idolaters – and our own lives 250 years on? The reverence for books has largely disappeared. In the Ayrshire town of Irvine, where Burns was introduced to the Scots ballads by the local bookseller, it is no longer possible to buy a book – there is no commercial source. Here in Kilmarnock, where I write this, the town in which Burns had his first edition printed, W H Smith hangs on, promoting the usual collections of cookery recipes, but there is no proper bookshop. It is drearily the same in most Scottish towns. Meanwhile, the public libraries, many created by philanthrophy, including the Carnegie library in Burns's home town, have been starved of resources and present a sad sight. Such thirst for knowledge as we have seems to be satisfied by the anarchic internet, not by the object considered sacred by the child Robert.

Despite our many privileges, the reverence for learning seems also to have gone. R F Mackenzie, whose book *A Search for Scotland* should be a standard text in every secondary school (but I am sure isn't), promoted the heretical belief that it was the policy of successive governments not to educate children. In tenacious pursuit of this policy, successive governments have built a national network of monstrous prison schools, some housing as many as 2,000 inmates, who are expected to pass as many exams as possible in the ludicrous belief that this will somehow equip them for 'real life', whatever that is. We no longer belt them for failing to sing the psalms to their teacher's satisfaction. The cruelties are subtler now.

They then proceed, most of the inmates of the prison schools, to some form of higher education, producing at the end of the experience a 'dissertation' full of received wisdom, or lack of it, and from which all original thought has been excised in advance.

Call this education? Burns was the lucky one. Robert Burns, then, is not one of us. He is not wandering around Irvine or Kilmarnock looking in vain for a bookshop. He is not surfing the web. He is not condemned to one of the prison schools. He is not writing a dissertation. He is not a product of the Scottish educational 'system'. He is not watching reality TV in a darkened living room. He is not in a pub, staring dully at a screen. He is not addicted to football. He is not attending Burns suppers. For all these reasons, and thousands more, he is not one of us. He is worth rather better than us. He is that free spirit we should dare to call an artist.

22 January 2009

Birthdays 2

Last days of a poet

Catherine Czerkawska

At Brow Well on the Solway, you walk to the very edge of the land and almost tumble into a mass of thrift, clumps of pink flowers fringing the shore, like some wild garden. They face the sea, looking outwards and when the wind blows through them, they tremble with a dry, feathery sound.

At all times of the year, the wind blows unhindered across these mudflats. There is nothing to stop it, down here, on the Solway. And the sky is dazzling: high and bright with the malicious glitter of a sun half hidden behind clouds. It is a place of endings, of dizzying infinities. A place where long horizontals constantly carry the eye outwards and beyond. Where these same long horizontals dull the urge to fly.

In June, when the thrift is still in bloom, it is as restful as it will ever be. There are wild roses in the hedgerows, white, pale and dark pink. There is a froth of bramble flowers with the promise of fruit to come. Oystercatchers and peewits patrol the mud. There are whaups bubbling in the peaty wastes. And you can hear the laverock, climbing higher and higher, to the very edges of sound and tumbling through the skies in an ecstasy of movement. Down there, in front of you, a burn meanders through the mud, fresh water meeting salt, while beyond that again is more mud and silver water, cloud shadows and the misty hills of another country. But it is still the loneliest sight you will ever see.

On the third of July in the year 1796, Robert Burns left his home in Dumfries and travelled to Brow Well on the Solway. It was, essentially, a poor man's spa. There was a chalybeate or mineral spring with a stone tank built to house it and not much else. One Doctor Maxwell had diagnosed a wholly fictional malady called flying gout, and advised him to drink the waters in an effort to alleviate his symptoms. He was thin, he was weak, he could barely eat and he was in constant pain. He stayed in a cottage close by. He ate a little thin porridge, and drank some porter with milk in it. When the porter bottle was empty, he told his landlady that the 'muckle black deil' had got into his wallet, and asked her if she would accept his personal seal as payment but she refused it and brought him the porter anyway.

In July, the thrift would have been dying. As well as instructing him to drink the foul tasting waters, the doctors had recommended that Robert should try seabathing. They were only following the fashion of the time. In the south of England there would have been snug bathing machines and separate beaches for men and women to indulge in the novelty of salt water against skin. One month's bathing in January was thought to be more efficacious than six months in summer. But perhaps there was a sense of urgency in the poet's case. No time to wait for winter.

He was, no doubt, in that state of desperation where you will try anything. He would have gone struggling and staggering and wading into the sea, half a mile every day, far enough for the water to reach up to his waist, because that's what the doctors had advised. Did they know how shallow these waters were? How far he would have to walk? How bitter the struggle for desperate mind over failing flesh? His landlady would have gone flounder trampling when she was a lassie, kilting her skirts up and wading out into the firth, feeling for the fishes with her toes. Did he feel the Solway flounders slithering away beneath his unsteady feet? It was his last chance of a cure and he was full of fear. Fear for his wife who was heavily pregnant. Fear of debt. Fear of death.

Nearby is the village of Ruthwell. In the church, there is an Anglo Saxon cross. It is so tall that the floor has been dug out to make room for it. Because it was judged an idolatrous monument with its intricate carving, its runic inscriptions, which must have seemed suspiciously pagan, it was smashed into pieces on the orders of the General Assembly of the Church of Scotland. That was in 1664, but it lay where it fell for many years and the good folk of Ruthwell used the stone blocks as benches to sit upon, while they yawned their way through interminable sermons. They had to destroy it where it stood, because the cross was there long before the kirk, which was built around it, an irony which seems to have been lost on these stone killers, as they were sometimes called. They would light fires beneath the stone and pour cold water on the cracks until they split apart.

Later the pieces were removed into the churchyard, which was where the poet may have seen them. In 1818, one Henry Duncan gathered the fragments together and restored the whole. The runes are a quotation from a powerful Anglo Saxon poem called *The Dream of the Rood*. It is a poem in two voices – the dreamer who relates his dream and the voice of the cross itself, telling how he – or perhaps she, for there is a certain sexual element in the poem – was cut down in the forest, how the young hero was sacrificed, struggling in blood and pain upon the body of the tree, both of them victims of a savage betrayal. *Rod wæs ic ar#red. Ahof ic ricne cyning.* A cross I was raised. I lifted the mighty king on high. The poet's voice calls to us down the years but only if we are willing to listen.

The seawater would have done some good only in that it numbed the pain. In July at Brow Well on the Solway, you can still hear how the laverocks climb to the very edges of sound while at his feet there would be the silvery meander of a burn finally finally. It would have been his last chance.

He had been a week at the salt water and had secret fears that this business would be dangerous if not fatal. No flesh or fish could he swallow. Porridge and milk and porter were the only things he could taste. And how could he attempt horseriding, which the doctors had also ordered, when he could not so much as drag himself up into the saddle?

'God help my wife and children if I am taken from their head with Jean eight months gone,' he wrote. He sent letters to his father-in-law, Adam Armour, begging him to let Jean's mother come to Dumfries, but there was only silence from Mauchline. His correspondence reeks of desperation.

From the middle of the month, the tides were unsuitable for bathing, so he went home, borrowing a gig from a farmer named John Clark, in Locharwoods. When he got back to Dumfries, he was too weak to walk up the Mill Vennel, let alone climb the stairs to his bed.

Poor Burns had almost run his course. Still, he must struggle with the stream, till some chopping squall overset the silly vessel at last. Love swells like the Solway but ebbs like the tide. Life too. And all the sweet waters flowing by, the bonnie banks and green braes, all the soft flesh, pressed close, all these things come only to love. The greatest of these is love.

It is not hard to see these things, here at Brow Well, on the Solway. He walks to the sea, and comes to the edge of the land and almost falls into a great mass of thrift, clumps of pink, fringing the shore like some wild garden. But it is already dying. You can picture him. You can see him in your mind's eye, as he goes struggling and staggering and wading through the water. It is July. The wind blows unhindered across the mudflats. And the sky is dazzling: high and bright with the malicious glitter of a sun half hidden behind clouds.

You come to the edge of the land. The thrift fringes the shore like some wild garden. But it is already fading to brown. When the wind blows through the flowers, they tremble, with a dry, feathery sound. You walk to the sea and there are laverocks singing. Who knows where sky ends and sea begins or where sea dissolves into sand? This is a place of endings, a place of infinities. The birds are so high you can hardly hear them. They climb to the very edges of sound. Like his words in her mouth, his Jean, like his songs on her lips. And at his feet the silvery meander of a burn. He, who always sang of rivers and streams, is coming, at last, to the sea.

5 May 2009

Birthdays 3

And then we sever

Barbara Millar

The 25th of January may have passed, but 2009 also marks the 250th anniversary of the birth of Robert Burns' most celebrated muse – Clarinda – perhaps the only woman he loved but never bedded.

Agnes Craig was born in Glasgow on 20 April 1759 (although some have suggested she may have been born in 1758 but knocked a year off her age, to appear younger than Burns). Her father was Andrew Craig, son of a Glasgow merchant, who had been elected to the Faculty of Physicians and Surgeons in Glasgow in 1745 and, in 1746, was made town surgeon on a salary of £10 a year, supplemented by lucrative private patients. Craig and his wife lived in the Saltmarket. Agnes was their fifth child, but she and her sister Margaret were the only ones to survive infancy. Agnes was also the great-niece of celebrated Scottish mathematician Colin MacLaurin (who until recently held the record as the world's youngest professor).

Her father had vehemently opposed the match with James McLehose, a Glasgow law agent, often described as 'dissolute', 'drunken', 'a wastrel' and 'brutish', and forbade the young man to enter his house. But McLehose determined to pursue Agnes and, on one occasion, when he knew Agnes would be travelling from Glasgow to Edinburgh, bought up all the other seats in the coach, so that he would be her sole travelling companion.

In the end her father did give her away in marriage and she had four children by McLehose in four years, one of the babies dying in infancy. In 1780, terrorised by a turbulent, violent marriage during which she was regularly beaten, Agnes fled to her father's home while McLehose set sail for Jamaica, although the couple never divorced. Two years later her father, who had been in ill health for some time, died, leaving Agnes with the rents on some property in Glasgow, which were sold to provide her with an annuity, and £50 in the bank. Craig stipulated in his will that none of his effects should ever come into the hands of James McLehose.

Agnes McLehose, often also known by the diminutive 'Nancy', moved to Edinburgh to 'a desolate-looking court of ancient buildings' in Potterrow, in the Old Town. The court was known as the General's Entry and it was claimed the accommodation had once been assigned to General Monk, while commanding in Scotland, though there was little evidence to support this. The buildings were erected by James Dalrymple, afterwards the first Earl of Stair, and Monk was a frequent visitor to his friend – which may have been how the rumour that Monk lived there began. Nancy moved in to 'a little parlour, bedroom and kitchen' in the court, living on her annuity which was supplemented, from time to time, by gifts from her cousin, Lord Craig.

On 4 December 1787 Nancy met Robert Burns at a tea party in the house of Miss Erskine Nimmo in Alison Square, Edinburgh. Nancy had been urging Miss Nimmo to effect an introduction to the celebrated young poet for some time as a letter to Burns after the tea party reveals: 'Miss Nimmo can tell you how earnestly I had long impressed her to make us acquainted. I had a presentiment that we should derive pleasure from the company of each other'.

Burns and Nancy were instantly attracted to each other and Nancy went home and penned a note, inviting him to tea the following week. He was unable to make that day but offered to come two days later. However, in the intervening period, the actions of a drunken coachman caused Burns to fall from a coach and sustain 'a good, serious, agonising, damn'd, hard knock on the knee'. His doctor would not allow him to move; he was confined to his lodging. Thus began his correspondence with Nancy.

'I can say with truth, Madam, that I never met with a person in my life whom I more anxiously wished to meet again than yourself...I know not how to account for it.' Nancy replied in kind: 'I perfectly comprehend...'

She then sent him some of her verse, which he praised as 'poetry, and good poetry', and at Christmas they exchanged further poems. By this time they had decided to give themselves pseudonyms – she was 'Clarinda', Burns 'Sylvander' – but the correspondence was taking an amorous turn, which Nancy could ill-afford to indulge. Her Calvinistic spiritual adviser, Rev John Kemp of the Tolbooth Kirk, and her benefactor, Lord Craig, would scarcely have approved of a married woman exchanging flirtatious missives and she urged Burns: 'I entreat you not to mention our corresponding to anyone on earth. Though I've conscious innocence, my situation is a delicate one.'

On 5 January 1788, Burns was able to visit Nancy in a sedan chair. There followed a further five visits during the month. After his visit on 12 January, she wrote: 'I will not deny it, Sylvander, last night was one of the most exquisite I ever experienced. Few such fall to the lot of mortals! Few, extremely few, are formed to relish such refined enjoyment. But though our enjoyment did not lead beyond the limits of virtue, yet today's reflections have not been altogether unmixed with regret.' Burns reassured her: 'I would not purchase the dearest gratification on earth, if it must be at your expense in worldly censure; far less, inward peace.'

She clearly was uncomfortable following further meetings, writing: 'I am neither well nor happy. My heart reproaches me of last night. If you wish Clarinda to regain her peace, determine against everything but what the strictest delicacy warrants.' 'Clarinda, my life, you have wounded my soul,' responded Burns and, shortly afterwards, the relationship began to decline.

Burns had an affair with a servant girl (possibly Nancy's own servant), Jenny Clow, who later bore him a son. Just before he left Edinburgh in February 1788, heading via Glasgow, Paisley and Kilmarnock, to Mossgiel and, ultimately, a marriage to the patient Jean Armour, there was a further exchange of letters between the two, with Burns apologising for the 'injury' Sylvander had caused Clarinda's reputation.

They corresponded a little during 1790 and met, for the last time, in Edinburgh on 6 December 1791. On 27 December Burns sent Nancy the bitter-sweet love poem *Ae Fond Kiss*. The next month she boarded a ship for Jamaica, to attempt a reconciliation with her husband, only to discover that he had replaced her with a mistress who had borne him a daughter. She returned to Scotland three months later and, although a few friendly letters were exchanged with Burns, his passion for her was extinguished. His final letter was sent on 25 June 1794.

Thirty five years later, on the anniversary of his death, Nancy wrote in her diary: 'This day I can never forget. Parted with Burns in the year 1791, never more to meet in this world. Oh, may we meet in Heaven!' Nancy McLehose died in 1841, aged 82 years. Her correspondence with Burns – some 80 letters between Sylvander and Clarinda – was valued at £25 at her death. She was buried in the Canongate kirkyard in Edinburgh, where a celebrated bronze sculpture to her 'voluptuous loveliness' stands against the eastern wall.

27 January 2009

Birthdays 4

Darwin in Scotland

P J B Slater

It will not have escaped the notice of many people that this year is a special one as far as the memory of Charles Darwin is concerned. A spate of conferences, exhibitions and programmes on radio and television is taking place in his honour, and many more books are being added to shelves already pretty full with those both by and about him. The reasons are twofold: he was born 200 years ago, on February 12 1809, and it is 150 years since his great work *The Origin of Species* was published.

Darwin was not honoured by the nation in his lifetime: were it not for his honorary LLD from Cambridge, he would have died simply Mr Darwin FRS. He suffered from chronic ill-health and, after his return from the voyage of the Beagle and marriage to his cousin Emma Wedgwood, ventured rather seldom from their home at Down House in Kent. Yet he received a state funeral when he died, and was buried in Westminster Abbey. Few biologists would now dissent from the view that 'The Origin' is the most important book ever published in their subject. That large numbers of people fail to accept its message says more for their lack of biological education than for the existence of room for doubt.

Darwin was very much an English gentleman, his father a doctor who lived outside Shrewsbury, his mother a member of the Wedgwood pottery family. Apart from his five years on the Beagle, much of his life was spent in Kent. So where does the Scottish connection come in? It does so in two interesting ways. First, from periods of time that he spent in Scotland and their influence upon him, and second through the intellectual precursors that he had north of the border. Nothing in this world is new and, while Darwin described the theory of evolution by natural selection in great detail and amassed a huge amount of evidence for it, there are earlier glimpses of similar ideas, and several of their authors were Scots.

Charles Darwin's first period in Scotland was in 1825-27, when he spent some 18 months studying medicine in Edinburgh. His elder brother Erasmus, who was in Cambridge also studying medicine, was able to spend a period doing hospital work in Edinburgh and the two of them shared lodgings at 11 Lothian Street, a building now demolished but, perhaps appropriately, replaced by new natural science galleries of the Royal Museum. A plaque in Charles' honour is mounted above the door.

Charles did not enjoy his medical studies. He was squeamish at the sight of blood and the sight of an operation without anaesthetic caused him to rush from the room. He was far from complimentary in his comments on several of the lecturers. But his interest in natural history was already well established. He spent many hours on the foreshore of the Forth, venturing even on a trip to the Isle of May, and became firm friends with Robert Grant, an austere man some years his senior, expert on sponges and with some evolutionary ideas of his own, who later became a professor of zoology in London. So, though he was patently unsuited to medical studies, and moved on to read theology in Cambridge, Darwin's time in Edinburgh was not wasted. He heard Audubon lecture and attended a meeting of the Royal Society of Edinburgh with Sir Walter Scott in the chair. In his autobiography he clearly looked back on his time there with affection when he commented that no similar honours had given him more pleasure than honorary membership of that society and of the undergraduate Royal Medical Society at Edinburgh University, both accorded to him later in life. But medicine was clearly not for him.

To my knowledge Charles Darwin only paid one other visit to Scotland and this was in 1838, shortly after his return from the voyage on the Beagle. He travelled to Glen Roy, near Spean Bridge, to examine the famous 'parallel roads', three lines that run round the hillside high above the valley floor. These were a source of controversy, some even arguing that they were evidence for Noah's flood. But Darwin thought otherwise: he subsequently wrote a paper suggesting that they were beaches which had become high and dry because the land had risen, a geological phenomenon he had observed in South America. Later studies, notably by Louis Agassiz, pointed to a different conclusion: a plug at the entrance to the valley had sealed in a body of water, and these were evidence of its level at three different times.

When Thomas Jamieson, an Ellon farmer and later lecturer in agriculture at the University of Aberdeen, wrote to him in 1861 with observations in support of this idea, Darwin was convinced. 'I give up the ghost,' he replied, 'My paper is one long gigantic blunder...How rash it is in science to argue because any case is not one thing, it must be some second thing that happens to be known to the writer.'

Neither of Darwin's visits to Scotland was, therefore, a great success. But what then of evolutionary thinking north of the border? Ideas about evolution certainly had quite common currency well before 'The Origin'. His own grandfather, an earlier Erasmus, had written on the subject. Others, such as Charles's Edinburgh mentor Robert Grant, were attracted by Lamarck's views on the inheritance of acquired characteristics. But what of the key idea of natural selection? Most famously, this was hit upon at around the same time by Alfred Russel Wallace, whose letter to Darwin outlining the idea is credited with spurring the great man to get 'The Origin' into print. But natural selection too had its earlier proponents, though none wrote of it in detail and most shied clear of taking it to its logical conclusion, probably for fear of antagonising church authorities. It might explain varieties within a species, but it was dangerous to suggest that it might go further.

Somewhat remarkably, a high proportion of this band of Darwinian precursors were Scots. The most colourful of these was undoubtedly James Burnett, Lord Monboddo, a somewhat eccentric judge who loved to be controversial and argued for the common descent of man and apes. His main study was, however, of languages, and he was one of the founders of comparative linguistics. The idea of natural selection was implicit in his view of language evolution and in his *Origin and Progress of Man and Language* (1773) he argued for a single origin and subsequent radiation for languages and likewise for human races. In 1875, Charles Neaves wrote the following rhyme in his honour:

Though Darwin now proclaims the law
And spreads it far abroad, O!
The man that first the secret saw
Was honest old Monboddo.

James Hutton, often credited with being the father of modern geology, was another precursor. He wrote a great deal, much of it not easy reading, but there is, in his *Investigation of the Principles of Knowledge* (1794), a brief (if somewhat ponderous) summary of natural selection:

'...if an organised body is not in the situation and circumstances best adapted to its sustenance and propagation, then, in conceiving an indefinite variety among the individuals of that species, we must be assured, that, on the one hand, those which depart most from the best adapted constitution, will be the most liable to perish, while, on the other hand, those organised bodies, which most approach to the best constitution for the present circumstances, will be best adapted to continue, in preserving themselves and multiplying the individuals of their race.'

William Wells, who was born in South Carolina of Scots parents, but returned to Scotland to be educated, first in Dumfries and then at Edinburgh University, had much the same idea for the races of mankind. In an appendix to his *Two Essays* (1818) he referred to the artificial selection of animal breeds by humans and wrote that it:

'...seems to be done with equal efficiency, though more slowly, by nature, in the formation of varieties of mankind, fitted for the country which they inhabit. Of the accidental varieties of man, which would occur among the first scattered inhabitants, some one would be better fitted than the others to bear the diseases of the country. This race would multiply while the others would decrease, and as the darkest would be the best fitted for the [African] climate, at length [they would] become the most prevalent, if not the only race.'

Even more impressively, but locked away in a book *On Naval Timber and Arboriculture* (1831), Patrick Matthew, a fruit farmer from the Carse of Gowrie, wrote:

'There is a law universal in nature, tending to render every reproductive being the best possible suited to its condition that its kind, or organised matter, is susceptible of, which appears intended to model the physical and mental or instinctive powers to their highest perfection and to continue them so. This law sustains the lion in his strength, the hare in her swiftness, and the fox in his wiles. As nature, in all her modifications of life, has a power of increase far beyond what is needed to supply the place of what falls by Time's decay, those individuals who possess not the requisite strength, swiftness, hardihood, or cunning, fall prematurely without reproducing – either a prey to their natural devourers, or sinking under disease, generally induced by want of nourishment, their place being occupied by the more perfect of their own kind, who are pressing on the means of subsistence.'

If one has a good idea, it pays to publish where people may read it. Unsurprisingly, Darwin had not come across this until Matthew, reading a review of 'The Origin' in The Gardener's Chronicle, wrote to the magazine to draw attention to it. Darwin replied, referring to Matthew's account as 'a complete but not developed anticipation' of his own ideas.

Perhaps the most successful Scot to have evolutionary ideas before Darwin was Robert Chambers, co-founder with his brother of the publishing house of that name. His *Natural History of the Vestiges of Creation* (1841), originally anonymous but attributed to him after his death (he had a reputation to protect), sold more copies in the 19th century than 'The Origin'. In it, he suggested that everything currently in existence, from planets to people, had developed by transmutation from earlier forms. The book was well written and in a popular style, but not well argued, inaccurate in many ways and lacking in convincing evidence. Unlike the others I have mentioned above and, of course, most convincingly Darwin and Wallace, he also failed to hit upon the crucial idea of natural selection.

In 1845 Darwin wrote that the author's 'geology strikes me as bad, and his zoology far worse'. In an historical sketch which he included in later editions of 'The Origin' he wrote of Vestiges: 'In my opinion it has done excellent service in this country in calling attention to the subject, in removing prejudice, and in thus preparing the ground for the reception of analogous views.' Somewhat faint praise.

Given that Scotland in general and Edinburgh in particular was in many ways the intellectual capital of the world in the late 18th and early 19th century it is perhaps not surprising to find there a disproportionate number of evolutionary thinkers in the pre-Darwinian period. Though Darwin was doubtless unaware of most of their writings when he wrote the first edition of 'The Origin', he must have been exposed to many such ideas earlier, particularly during his period in Edinburgh. His conversations with Robert Grant, and discussions at the debating societies to which he belonged while there, would all have been an important part of his intellectual development. But, in recognising natural selection as being the prime force in evolution, in amassing the huge body of incontrovertible evidence necessary to make that case, and in his courage to stand up against the established order, Charles Darwin really does have to be the most revolutionary biologist of all time. Only by him was this beautiful idea really nailed to the mast.

6 July 2009

Part VIII

Brief lives

Brief lives 1

Notes on a scandal

Ian Mackay

I am enjoying 'Islay McLeod's Scotland' and found her photo features on the north coast brought back memories of my time working as a ghillie at the House of Tongue in student summer holidays for three years in the late 1960s.

The house was let each August to the Longman family (of publishing fame) who invited some of their more successful clients and friends. I was ghillie, relief gardener, handyman, dishwasher, shopper, etc and generally on hand to ensure everyone enjoyed their holiday. There are several occasions I remember in particular:

Taking Ludovic Kennedy out for five hours' loch fishing when we covered so many topics including his career, the state and future of the Highlands and politics generally. He talked about his switch from the Liberals to SNP which I had not been aware of but in Tongue I did not have access to radio or television and rarely saw a newspaper (they did not arrive there until 5.30pm). A couple of months later, back in Edinburgh, I heard him give a speech in which he announced his switch and it was headline news the next day. I had had an exclusive two months earlier and did not realise it.

His wife, Moira Shearer, was there also, with their children. She had given up her highly successful ballet career to look after the family. She was about 40 when I met her and even to someone still in his teens she was stunning with her red hair, wonderful figure and friendly personality. For grouse shooting we used two pointer dogs, one of which roamed the hill picking up grouse scent while I held the other on a lead to give it a rest. In addition to dealing with the dogs I carried the game bag and any jackets if it was hot. Moira was the only guest ever to offer to take the dogs. When I had two strong dogs on a Y-shaped lead life was fine if they pulled in opposite directions, but if they set off with a common aim across the old peat hags, mud up to the knees was often the result for the poor dog handler. She was determined to take the dogs despite my warnings and off she went leaping over any obstacles with such poise.

Taking William Douglas Home, brother of Sir Alec and a successful playwright at that time, fishing and him not catching anything for hours. That evening one of his plays was opening in the West End and he was naturally anxious. To keep his spirits up he burst into song, at the top of his voice, singing 'When I'm 64'.

Shooting with Richard Beaumont, chairman of Purdey guns, who had great tales of having to go with an engineer to fix guns for some of their more influential clients such as various Russian leaders and Franco.

The Longmans used Sir Gordon Richards to train their horses and he used to phone any time one of their horses ran, to explain why it had lost and how it would do better next time. He usually called when the family was out and my girlfriend (long since my wife), who had a summer job as a housemaid, usually took his calls and passed on all his excuses to the family.

Going to the local shop for groceries and having to wait from 11.00 to 11.15am while all the staff had their tea break.

Being quizzed by the shop owner on what brands of luxury foods they had brought from Harrods. Within days he would have these on his shelves, they would spot them and decide that next time they could get these in Tongue. My reward was a Mars bar.

Taking the mail to the Post Office in the morning to catch the mail bus and being given the job of franking them while the postmistress read the post cards.

Seeing the best display of the northern lights imaginable.

Being probably the only Mackay to celebrate his 21st birthday in the clan seat since it was sold to the Sutherlands in 1829. As one day seemed to roll into the next I had forgotten about my birthday until the postie brought my cards at 5.30pm.

Jack Profumo and family were regular guests at the House of Tongue in the early 1960s and when the affair with Christine Keeler hit the headlines they sought refuge there. As they were very well liked in the area the locals discouraged the press pack as much as they could, mainly by not offering accommodation and by leading them on wild goose chases. A few nights sleeping in their cars, no sightings and no stories and most of them departed. My first year there was roughly when his brother-in-law bought an estate in east Sutherland and for years after the family holidayed there, making regular visits to Dornoch Cathedral. He was in the congregation when my daughter was christened in 1975.

But it was not all idyllic. One of my phobias is handling a bird, alive or dead, so catching and dealing with an injured grouse was an ordeal and cleaning them was even worse but fortunately after the first day of the season I could cope. I once spoke to a careers advisor about how I could get into land management so I could live in somewhere like Tongue (is there anywhere like Tongue?) but without an agricultural background I had to forget it. So Tongue became a host of great experiences and Dornoch is not that far away from it.

26 August 2008

Brief lives 2

The modest VC

Sheila Hetherington

I

We knew him as the tall, dark-haired treasurer of the Scots Kirk in Bombay (in daily life a senior member of staff at Grindlay's Bank). People, gathering to chat outside church after the morning service, would murmur to each other as he approached, 'Look, here comes Ian Cruickshank. He's a VC, but he's so modest – no-one would ever know!'

Ian and his Canadian wife were a popular and established part of the gregarious Scottish circle when we arrived. Celebrations included Burns nights, St Andrew's nights, reels danced out on the maidan at the Gymkhana Club. (I remember one that began as an eightsome, broke into a sixteensome, and eventually ended as a slightly chaotic 128-some, without pause).

Due to Ian's personal modesty, we never came to know what he had done to earn his decoration, and quite soon we moved to Africa, regretfully leaving friends and acquaintances, losing touch, in the way that one does.

Many years later I found out about Ian. Alastair and I were exploring Shetland. We visited Yell, where they were holding a retrospective wartime exhibition. There, on one of the screens, was Ian's story, which must already be familiar to many.

Early in 1944, flying officer John Cruickshank, with part of 210 squadron coastal comand, was posted to Sullom Voe in Shetland, on anti-U boat and general maritime reconnaissance duties in northern waters. He was pilot of a Catalina flying boat, an aircraft that was proving vital to the RAF in defending British convoys from the constant menace of German U-boat attack.

On 17 July/18 July 1944, while on anti-submarine patrol north west of the Norwegian Lofoten Islands, flying officer Cruickshank and his crew spotted a German U-boat. Despite fierce anti-aircraft fire, John launched an attack. A German shell exploded inside the aircraft, killing the navigator and injuring several members of the crew. Cruickshank himself was struck in 72 separate places, including two serious wounds to his lungs and severe injuries to his legs.

Despite damage to his aircraft and with several crew members badly injured, Cruickshank pressed home the attack. On the first attempt the depth charges failed to drop, but Cruickshank made a second run, before releasing the depth charges himself, in the absence of his dead navigator. This time the attack was successful. The depth charges hit their target, sinking the U-boat.

Cruickshank collapsed, and the controls were taken over by another member of the crew, but shortly afterwards he recovered somewhat and, bleeding profusely, insisted on taking control once more. Only when he was sure that the aircraft was airworthy and the homeward course plotted and set, would he relinquish command and consent to have his wounds attended to. He refused to be given morphia, however, for fear that it might prevent him from the responsibilty of supervising the remaining five and a half hours of the flight. Throughout the journey back he lapsed in and out of consciousness.

The aircraft made it back to its Shetland base, but it was in such a dangerous condition that landing it would be a severe test for the wounded co-pilot. Cruickshank insisted on being carried forward to the co-pilot's seat, from which he gave orders, refusing to allow a landing until sea conditions had quietened sufficiently. After circling for an hour, he helped to bring the sea-plane in for a safe landing on water, ensuring that it was beached where it could easily be retrieved and collected for repair. It was only then that Cruickshank collapsed. He was given a blood transfusion before he was removed to hospital

John Cruickshank demonstrated remarkable skill, courage and determination in appalling circumstances. Thanks to him and his second pilot, flight sergeant Garnett, the aircraft was able to destroy an enemy submarine and return to base. Garnett received the DFM for his part in the operation. Two other members of the crew were also decorated.

To his own astonishment – he had never expected a decoration – John Cruickshank's VC for conspicuous bravery was gazetted in September 1944.

II

It seems inappropriate to follow that tale of superb gallantry with a slightly harum-scarum anecdote of my own, in which, although he is unaware of it, Ian played a crucial role. We never met again, but whenever I see him being honoured on television, I smile, and remember how grateful I am that I once knew him.

We had been living in Lahore for a relatively short time, but were due to leave. Because we had two little daughters, we could not travel together, but Hamish suggested that before leaving the sub-continent for ever, we should each, separately, do something we really wanted to do. He chose to go up to the North West Frontier. I decided to visit the Taj by moonlight – something of a cliché, of course – and something that I understand is no longer possible, as nowadays the Taj may only be visited during daylight hours. I planned my trip to last over three days, coinciding with a full moon.

Relations between Pakistan and India were bad at the time, but the travel agent in Lahore booked my hotel, cheerfully assuring me that I could take exchangeable currency, and that their counterparts in Delhi would also cash a UK cheque, if needed. I was, then, not unduly troubled when Pakistani customs took all my rupees (for collection on return), knowing that I would be able to get cash next morning.

On my evening arrival in Delhi, I borrowed money from a trusting desk clerk at the hotel, and paid my taxi-driver. Early next morning I presented myself at the travel agents, who politely but firmly refused to cash my UK cheque. I wandered disconsolately round the streets of Delhi, considering my predicament. Communication with Pakistan had been cut off, so it was not possible to phone. I now owed money to the desk clerk, and even if I spent nothing more, I would have a three-night hotel bill to pay before flying home. I seemed to be in a bit of trouble: in fact at that moment life seemed to be somewhat bleak.

I chose the largest branch of Lloyds Bank and asked to see the manager. I was ushered in to the presence of a kindly Welshman, who listened to my problem, but then explained that – with regret – he was unable to help, as he had no idea who I might be:

an understandable difficulty, as I acknowledged. He was sympathetic, though, and we chatted for a while. I happened to mention that we had lived in Bombay at one time, and he was immediately interested. He asked if I could remember any of our friends there. Some divine inspiration made me mention Ian Cruickshank's name. He brightened up at once. 'Ah well now, if you know Ian Cruickshank, how much do you want?' Oh, blessed blessed Ian!

6 November 2008

Islay McLeod's Scotland

Kitchen workers, Merchant City, Glasgow

Top: Central Station,
Saturday evening
Right: Mitchell Lane
Opposite top: snooker room
Opposite bottom: Union Street

Busker, Exchange Square

Central Station, Sunday morning

Summer, Skara Brae

Autumn, Fife

Top: Fishing for crabs, Lower Largo
Bottom: The cat of Ceres

Scenes from a European market, Dunfermline

Freedom

Brief lives 3

The forgotten nationalist

Andrew Hook

BBC2 Scotland's Scottish history series recently did us proud with an excellent programme about one of Scotland's strangely neglected public figures: R B Cunninghame Graham. Our neglect of Graham has always puzzled me. Here is a man who over a long career became a dominant figure in both British politics and British literature and yet in Scotland it sometimes seems he's been airbrushed out of our history.

Consider first Cunninghame Graham's political career. Elected a radical Liberal MP for north-west Lanarkshire in the late 19th-century, he campaigned for home rule for Ireland, for a 10-hour time limit on the working day, for the rights of the 'have-nots' everywhere to justice and freedom, and for an end to the excesses of capitalism at home and imperialism abroad. No wonder he was a thorn in the flesh of the Liberal establishment. Sympathetic to the socialist principles of William Morris, he participated in the original 'Bloody Sunday' demonstration in Trafalgar Square in 1887, was beaten up by the police, and imprisoned for six weeks. He emerged from prison a working-class hero, and in due course became a founding president of the Scottish Labour Party.

Disillusioned with parliament as a force for change in society, for a time he retired from politics. In the 1920s, however, he returned to public life, this time as a founding president of the Scottish National Party. Despite all this, I don't think I've ever heard a Labour or nationalist politician refer to his name in public.

Why not? Well perhaps because Graham was a Harrow-educated son of the Scottish landowning class. The family may not have been particularly wealthy, but there was no question of their status among the Scottish lairds. Then again early in his life, Cunninghame Graham became a dashingly romantic figure, spending four years on the pampas of South America seeking his fortune as rancher, horse-dealer, and gaucho. (He was never to lose his 'Don Roberto' nickname.) One suspects that neither the Labour Party nor the nationalists were comfortable about acknowledging their debt to a romantic aristocrat.

Graham's literary fortune parallels his political one. Turning to writing after his initial political career in the early modern Edwardian period, he soon became a familiar figure in literary circles. Among his friends were George Bernard Shaw, Joseph Conrad, Ezra Pound, Ford Madox Ford, W H Hudson and Edward Garnett. He produced a large number of books in a range of modes: fiction, memoir, essay, history, autobiography. He translated from the Spanish and did much to open up the history of South America to English readers. Yet he was also very much a Scottish writer – one deeply opposed to the 'kailyard' account of Scottish life and letters, and one who in his best work often portrayed the Calvinist strain in the Scottish church as a dehumanising force in Scottish society. Still he is largely unread today. Even academia neglects him. The recent *Edinburgh History of Scottish Literature* makes only a single passing reference to him as an anti-kailyard figure, and manages to misspell his name in the index.

The BBC2 programme did not have much to say about Cunninghame Graham's writing career, but it was nonetheless a timely reminder of his eminence and achievements. My one disappointment was its failure to allude to one of the most admirable and defining moments in its subject's public career. So let me end by recording it here.

In November and December 1890, and in January 1891, the London Daily Graphic published three letters from Graham responding to the reports the paper carried on the final confrontation between the Lakota Sioux Indians and the US army at Pine Ridge, North Dakota. (In what became known as the Massacre at Wounded Knee, the 7th cavalry killed over 200 people, many of them women and children.) Graham's letters are masterpieces of irony, outrage, and anger; the barbarity of the events, and the hypocrisy that surrounds them, are denounced with equal power. For Graham the whole episode is an example of imperialistic real-politik of the most brutal and indefensible kind. In the final letter he even links the American

Indian's way of life with that of the Scottish Highlander before his final defeat at Culloden: 'It is as ridiculous to expect an Indian to love work as it would have been to expect a Highlander of the time of the '45 to take to type-writing rather than cattle-lifting as a means of subsistance.' But the letter's ending, with its allusion to Buffalo Bill's Wild West shows, is even more bitterly ironic:

'It seems a pity, too, to waste so many good Indians who might have been so advantageously used to turn honest pennies for enterprising showmen, if no other method of utilising them occurred to the great American Republic. However, I may be permitted to make my moan over the women and children at least, for I doubt much if they had committed any weightier crimes than the unpardonable one of living.'

15 January 2009

Brief lives 4

One man's demons

Walter Humes

The late Dame Thora Hird, who continued working as an actress to a ripe old age, used to say: 'It's not being old that stops you doing things, rather it's not doing things that makes you old'. I was reminded of this maxim as I attended the funeral of a friend and former colleague this week.

As a young man, John had led a very active and adventurous life. He was a keen sailor and served in the navy for a number of years, travelling all over the world. At the funeral some of his youthful exploits while at sea and onshore were recalled with affection, including his tendency to disregard the rules on occasion. When he returned to civilian life he trained as a youth worker and developed a lifelong commitment to ensuring that youngsters, particularly those from disadvantaged backgrounds, had every opportunity to do something useful with their lives. He later moved into higher education, helping to train the next generation of youth and community workers. He was a lively lecturer, full of fun and extremely popular with students, many of whom kept in touch after qualifying.

As the end of working life approached, the prospect of retirement did not appeal to John. His marriage had ended and he knew he would miss the demands of work, the daily exchanges and even the irritations that accompany any job. His earlier exploits meant that he had no desire to travel the world again. His one extravagance was a powerful car which he drove at reckless speed. He once scared the wits out of me by insisting on taking me for a spin in the latest model, reaching 100 mph within an alarmingly short time. As I pointed out later, it was just as well we were having lunch after the drive rather than before, otherwise I might have made a mess of the smart leather interior.

John aged quickly after retirement. He did not enjoy good health and after a bad fall his mobility was greatly reduced. Not surprisingly, he became a bit depressed. He also lost his faith. One day while reading the lesson in church, he suddenly thought: 'I don't believe this any more'. He wrote to the minister explaining what had happened. That same minister at his funeral said that they had remained good friends and whenever he visited John he was treated as hospitably as ever. In a very touching moment at the end of the service, the minister said that we had rightly been celebrating all the positive aspects of John's colourful personality – his warmth, his humour, his generosity – but that he also had a darker side. The sad thing was that he had found it difficult to talk about the demons that haunted him. In common with many people who provide support and inspiration to others, when it came to expressing his own needs he was at a loss how to proceed.

As I drove home, I reflected again on Dame Thora's words. One can see the commonsense in them but the brisk philosophy which they express may not connect with everyone's personal journey. In his final years John lost his appetite for life, partly because his capacity to 'do things' was impaired. But as the many people who attended his funeral would testify, what really mattered were those earlier years, filled with energy, commitment and good cheer: these were the qualities that lifted the spirits of those who were fortunate enough to know him.

15 January 2009

Part IX

Travel

Travel 1

England 1914

Robins Millar

In the first hours of World War I – August 1914 – a young Scottish journalist was pedalling through England on a cycling holiday. This is the diary of his journey.

Saturday:
Left Glasgow cycling at 2 o'clock. Pushed through Hamilton to Larkhall. Tremendous industry. Stupendous activity. Enormously productive county. One sees railways, coalpits, cornfields, forests, meadows and foundries, jostling one another within a mile of landscape. Colliers everywhere in dark jackets and dirty corduroys, tied at knees, cans in pockets, oil lamps in cups.

Industry gradually left behind; dawdles to Lesmahagow and dies away in a wilder country. Climbing road. Wide expanse. Breezy, glorious day of sun and breeze. Made poetry. Took ten at Lesmahagow. Quiet hamlet with nothing doing at all.

Set out for Abington, 14-and-a-half miles, Douglas halfway. Noble lord's seat somewhere about, imposing gateway, visible to the naked eye, 20 feet high, with expansive triangle before it, presumably for carriages, and interminable carriage drive vanishing through park. Whole district has taken aspect of a public park. Public road like avenue through Kelvingrove but scenery noble and on grander scale than any park I ever saw. Everything clipped and cultivated like private grounds with gardener in attendance. The very hillsides cropped bare and rolling in amiable dignity like lawns; the grass among the woods beside the road short, free from weeds and uncouth vegetation. Trees of every description majestical by the wayside in innumerable battalions.

Past this into wildest moorland, destitute of aught but heather and peat grass, courting couples and sheep. Couples cycled out several miles, left machines lying on road and sat a few yards up on grass in full view of public. Why this prominence? Is this to satisfy respectability? Is this the maiden's modesty here, her convention of self-protection, that she must not leave the haunts of men to do her courting even round the corner until an understanding is affected?

Soon not a house within miles. Rolling hills looming round the long long road. Here and there belts of woodland, here and there a farm. Why so few? Surely cultivation, if possible at odd intervals, is capable of extension. Suspect most of this dreary district could be put to use by careful handling, either in farming or afforestation.

Found Abington rather swanky and ran on to Crawford which is only a degree so. Pleasant company in lounge to whose converse I listened from depth of armchair without joining in. Four men, two ladies, commonplace people but in good spirits, laughing at mild witticisms. Lounge separated by red curtains from sitting room where party of local bowlers were celebrating match with neighbouring champions. Never realised before the sublimated seriousness which the game is capable of arousing, as reverential a matter as philosophy, theology or golf, especially when elevated to a loftier plane by spiritual stimulant and an emotional atmosphere of beer.

Sunday:
Left at 10 o'clock after breakfast. Chat with two territorials travelling south on motorcycles. A beautiful run through wild scenery to Beattock. Very few people. A few tramps with long overcoats (for sleeping out), bearded brown faces and gingerly gait, brown sackcloth bags containing their belongings slung over their shoulders. Local gypsies by the wayside performing moving toilet and talking a strange tongue, one of them a young girl of striking beauty with dark skin and fine black eyes. She was combing out her long thick wavy black hair and the rags she was dressed in failed to disguise her charm. The caravan was a primitive ancient-looking contrivance, very dirty and dark inside. They had camped beside the turn of a gaily-singing pebbly stream whose music no doubt charmed their slumbers.

A little ragged barefoot boy ran beside me down a hill, holding in his hands a packet of salt and a stick of toffee. I gave him my hand and speeded him on his way a hundred yards and he thanked me through his panting breath as we parted.

Many trains were passing laden with guns, horses and troops who waved khaki-sleeved arms through the windows as they sped by. I am told that over 70 were expected over the next 24 hours. The big guns looked very sinister on the trucks, sometimes veiled with waterproof covering but, for the most part, shamelessly displayed. The horses stared from their waggons pathetically. And as the men did not know where they were going they were in no better case. They threw postcards from the windows as they passed through stations, for people to forward.

I stopped two hours at Lockerbie to lunch at the Bluebell Hotel, then passed on from this empty little town to Ecclefechan where I reverently sought out Carlyle's burying place. It was a very simple red sandstone block between two white ones, enclosed in railings among the graves of local townspeople and peasant folk. 'Humilitate' is inscribed above the names of Thomas and his brother. The graveyard is very peaceful, the serene sunlit hills and dignified trees overwatching it. One could muse upon the man, his greatness, his work and his worth, fitly here.

Moving towards Gretna I soon had a glimpse over the Solway Firth on my right and a bustling breeze to stir my hair, with a view over Liddesdale to my left, level, fertile and green.

I crossed into England, resting to sketch the burn that makes the boundary and dawdled up the long straight road into Carlisle, refreshing myself from time to time with brambles at the wayside. After tea, I strolled over to a Socialist club where I was hospitably received and watched a game of skittle pool, conversing with a local town councillor in his shirt-sleeves behind the temperance bar. The last thing I saw at night after I had turned out my light was a band of recruits, 80-strong, marching up the street below my window.

Monday:
Amusing experience last night. Coming upstairs I noticed maid leaning over the banisters. Whenever she saw me she gave a squawk and scurried. Mistress came out and apologised. Maid

had seen a German coming up the stairs. 'They're seeing Germans all over the place here,' she said.

Hear of great crowds of motor lorries coming from Scotland for war, drivers being taken over by government. Liverpool man says at one time they stretched waiting for use, three miles in streets. He tells me also he heard of wounded coming into Leith. Also he has seen troop ships leaving Liverpool, destination unknown, two every day.

Left for Penrith in blazing sunshine. Hilly road. Delightful scenery. Had a conversation with a young German, ex-waiter from Glasgow, rusticating in remote village here with friend, till war is over.

Had most enjoyable light lunch at Penrith, tomato soup, bread and butter and ginger beer. Cycled on to Pooley Bridge and took steamer to Ullswater to Patterdale. Lovely sail. Set off over Kirkstone Pass for Windermere. Terrific climb, pushing bike several miles up steep winding incline. View glorious but so exhausted by perseverance necessary for progress could hardly enjoy it properly. Passed motor broken down by wayside which helped to cheer me up. Reached top at last. Raised a cheer and rushed for a drink at the inn.

Going down was like wine. Scorched at top speed. Enjoyed scenery now. Marvellous! Unbeatable. On right, high mountains. On left a precipice with peaceful pasture and meadow valley at bottom and steep abrupt mountain rising up out of it. Finest road scenery I have ever seen. Windermere Lake looked beautiful in calm evening light.

On to Kendal. Pleasant run. Set off after wash in a burn and mild lunch of couple of sandwiches for Kirkby Lonsdale. Miserable run. Heavy series of steep hills that necessitated walking. Evening came down and then night and I had no lamp. Dreary road. Final trial, free wheel began to tremble and bike became at times unmanageable. Fortunately, last four miles were downhill. Scorched in the dark, tyres ripping like mad on the road, wind whipping my face and lungs gulping in air. Exhilarated and inspiring. Reached Kirby Lonsdale just as chimes struck nine.

Tuesday:
Took bike round to have free wheel replaced and it was 11.30 before I was ready to start. Had a chat with housemaid who said she was leaving at the end of the month to join a panto company. Had travelled in Scotland in that line before. 'It's a wonder you never saw my name in the papers. Alice Alderson they call me. I get a guinea a week.' I admitted it was a wonder. Day was very hot but road uninteresting. No particular scenery except near Lancaster. Solaced myself on the moorland road with numerous brambles here and there among the hedges. Lunched at Lancaster. Uninteresting scenery to Blackpool. Most of it practically flat as a table. Something like Holland but without the windmills. Worth seeing in a way though monotonous. Wind kept blowing in my face and surface of road not too good.

Blackpool (40 miles) at 6 o'clock. Extraordinary place. Crowds, all from Lancashire. Huge tower, tapering into sky, built of girders. Gigantic wheel beside it, winding slowly round and round. Barrel organs. Trams. Motor omnibuses. Tradesmen in white jackets standing at doors of shops booming goods. Open air booths full of sweets and 'rock' in bars a foot long and inches thick, pink, yellow and blue. Booths with fruit. Booths with postcards, mineral waters, collar studs, toys. Oyster shops. Five pence ha'penny shops. Auction shops. Hawkers with coloured balloons, newspapers, matches. Carcases driven 'naked' in butchers' lorries. Enormous piers stretching out to sea. White sailed yachts, with owners in blue jerseys and trousers rolled up from barefeet inviting crowds to come for a sail. Promenade on the front of great width and apparently miles long, worth seeing from above in the evening when the sea is black and lights are shining in water and blazing on long pavements with couples walking briskly along in gay attire. The Palace (admission 6d), a music hall combined with picture house, waxworks exhibition, monkey house and lions in cages and a dancing hall. The last truly palatial. Gaudy decorations, mirrors and pillars. Large orchestra. Refreshment bars. Beautifully polished floor. Dignified MC. Free and easy conventions. Dancing all night.

It was amazing going round side streets in an evening. Boarding houses galore with tiny front plots in which visitors were sunning themselves on garden seats, papa, mama, big brother and sister and the baby. All the men in striped shirt sleeves, even when posing for the travelling photographer. All the ladies in recumbent and strikingly inelegant attitudes. Everybody apparently thoroughly content and enjoying holiday to the full.

Wednesday:
Left about 12 o'clock after a walk along esplanade. Sea very hazy and suggestive of heat. Morning crowds perambulating leisurely. Apparently no bathing but there is no beach. Was picked up by a young man a couple of miles outside the town, who accompanied me almost all the way. Most uninteresting scenery. Flat and dull to Preston. After that paved road all the way to Manchester. Some fine buildings in the middle of Preston. Barracks there which were empty. A few fine villas outside Bolton. Otherwise a most dreary prospect of paving stones, brick cottages, mill chimneys and railways for 20 miles. Arrived very tired at Manchester, stabled bike at left luggage office, took a room at Brunswick Hotel, got tea and set out to find A Falconer at Worsley Road, Winton. Forty minutes or more in tram. Difficulty in finding place; Angus away on holiday.

Disappointment. Hospitably received by his landlord and entertained for an hour or two. Back late to hotel.

Awakened at 6am by soldiers marching past with bugle band. They were going to Preston barracks. Back to bed and slept till 10. Found I have cold in head. Don't know how I got it. Shall hasten out of Manchester (which is a noisy black city and unprepossessing in extreme to individual in my condition) to the green country, Shropshire direction.

Thursday:
Felt bad all forenoon. Messed about wasting time. Had no stomach for cycling. Decided to take train as far as Northwich so had to wait till 3.45. Central station waiting room one of the dingiest spots on earth. Who expects better in Manchester?

Left Northwich 5 o'clock. Enjoyed cycling immediately. Ran along Chester Road to 13 miles from that historic town and struck off to Tarporley where I had tea. Two pleasures: I met two

Welshmen and I partook of the best penny custard I ever tasted.

Went on through Banbury (pretty church, quaint houses) to Whitchurch where I spent night. Delightful run in dusk through Cheshire hedges. Level fields on every side, quaint with trees of every shape, poplars rearing their graceful thin maidenly forms above hedge lines; cows browsing evening pastures; bats flitting; gossips chatting at wayside; clumps of foliage of every shape massed over the road as I sped swiftly through the silent scene.

Lamps were lighting as I swung into Whitchurch's narrow streets and after a clean up I strolled in the dark listening to the strange tongue of the inhabitants, watching boys conduct mimic skirmishes, receiving insight into local cookery (Yorkshire ducks alias spicy puddings) and drinking in peaceful country night.

Friday:
To Shrewsbury. The road turned aside through a jumbled little village with a substantial church that had planted itself right in front of the road so that one had to go round about it. I had to inquire the way several times. Once on the main road I had a pleasant run up and down quiet byways, singing at times till the cows moo-ed in answer, a questionable compliment. I stopped to refresh my throat, strained no doubt by vocal gymnastics, with plentiful sour blackberries from the hedges.

Shrewsbury was full of soldiers of the Cheshire Regiment who were marching and dawdling, running with pots and with kettles or driving motorcycles, swaggering, plodding wearily, lounging and flirting all over the streets. I saw several ancient houses with black beams and whitened walls. One, the Gateway House, dating from 1613 or thereabouts, formed an entrance (there was a huge studded door, flung back) into a cobbled court where stood several more modern dignified Georgian brick houses, with climbing creepers, many windows and clean frontages, delightful to survey.

There was a house wherein Henry VII had lodged before the Battle of Bosworth Field. But how petty became these mediaeval squabbles in this far-off perspective compared with the titanic upheavals of modern Europe, whose echoes and outer ripples were before the eye in even this tiny country township.

The next road was round Wenlock Edge, the outer end of

Wenlock Hills, to Ironbridge, a small collection of red brick houses at a river's brink. A hill of remarkable steepness led out of Ironbridge to Madeley, where there was a coalmine. Descending was, of course, more of a pleasure and I was on the way to Bridgnorth soon, enjoying particularly the tremendous poplars by the wayside, which had indeed been a feature of the road from Shrewsbury.

A fortunate hint of a shortcut led me by a back road that missed Bridgnorth to Hoccum Farm and there I settled in for the weekend. In the evening I was taken for a stroll by the two girls of the house and the dog to 'Hoccum Pool' and an early retiral proved welcome to my weary limbs, excusably tremulous after a week's cycling of about 320 miles.

To keep me in memory, I note the inmates of the house, Mr Logan (gey dour); Mrs Logan (shy, good-hearted, a doormat); Cyril Meredith, a farming pupil, father at farm five miles off in Clavering, boarding school education, Shropshire accent, red-faced, thin, big nose, modest, silent but pleasantly talkative alone, as are they all, curiously enough; Charlie, Irish cousin, tall but lame, shy, silent, probably a screw loose – it was Charlie who spoke of the four Providences of Ireland, meaning Provinces, the butt of the would-be wit of the house, scolded and insulted but neither to be cajoled nor threatened into doing a hand's turn of work, aged 21; Maggie Logan, a big, sonsy farmer's daughter with arms like a man, heavy-footed and loud-voiced, wears glasses, tries to sing occasionally but keeps to two notes, plays piano with elephantine delicacy, has been baulked in life's ambition of becoming an actress so is studying for medicine degree in Glasgow and, having been two months in Queen Margaret's, swanks about like a veteran, impudent in the extreme to everybody, especially mother and Charlie, but not to papa who seems to be a Turk for discipline, full of spirits which at present causes effervescence more of conceit than good-humoured fun; Frances Logan, called Frank, tall, good-looking and graceful but is aware of it, sleepy eyes, silent, small pitted mouth, manners to stranger exquisite, to mother, peevish, insolent and insufferable, has no great inclination to talk about anything in particular, seldom reads, a beauty whose charm intimacy dissipates forever.

They were busy making shirts for soldiers and the evidence of industry littered the room all day. Mrs Logan took me into Bridgnorth on Saturday and showed me the church, the castle broken down by Cromwell's cannon, the old town hall, the open market place, the views over the Severn Valley, the sword of the cavalier colonel killed in the churchyard, the curious 'lift' from low town to high town. We made purchases, visited an old Scots couple (retired farmer) and returned in time for early supper and bed.

Talk throughout the weekend was chiefly of the war, news coming in of German advance through Belgium and of impending battle at French frontier in which British troops are to participate.

Sunday:

I went to the congregational chapel with Mrs Logan, my first visit to church for about a year. I wrote letters. Mr and Mrs Gray came over from neighbouring farm. We had met them in Bridgnorth on Saturday. Curiously, I had met them at Mrs Wilson's in Sussex two years ago. They had removed to this district. Fine people. Mrs Logan, Mrs Gray and I went for a walk through the fields, passing cut crops lying golden and mellow, awaiting carting to the granary, the rich grassy meadows with their cows and sheep, the tall elm trees whose long shadows fell across the paths, and the silent stagnant pools whereon the moorhens skittered noisily, while rabbits and hares skipped across the path and clumsy partridges rose in convoys at our coming.

The girls went off to their room before eight so I was left alone to finish my letters and to seek repose at an early hour. On Monday morning I strolled into Bridgnorth and in the afternoon, a shower or two of rain having died away, paid a pleasant visit to the Grays' farm, driven in the 'float', a heavy cart for transporting calves etc to market, by Charlie.

I had been getting tired of the atmosphere of the house especially two things: the girls' bad breeding and unkind manner towards their mother and Charlie, and the ghastly silence at meal times, which was set as an example by the head of the house and religiously copied by the rest of the family. It was too funereal for my volatile holiday spirits. With a bracing of the heart, I contrived to take the plunge of a sudden adieu on Tuesday morning and with extreme joy fled from the farm as soon as breakfast was over. Mrs Logan, with all her shyness, reserve and inability to emotionalise, was kindness itself. The others were too egotistic.

Tuesday:
The wind was favourable again. My luck has been phenomenal. With one or two short exceptions it has helped me since I left Glasgow. I got to Kidderminster shortly after 10 o'clock. There was nothing to see so, pausing only to buy half a pound of yellow plums for a halfpenny, I pushed on to Droitwich, an old-fashioned little place full of those black and white cottages. I made a sketch and I sampled cider – horrid stuff, like vinegar – with regret, and made for Alcester, towards Shakespeare country. Here I dined and rested (in the Royal Oak). There is a delightful church and a general old English air about some parts of the town that made me think of the genial slow stilted and dignified days when Victoria came to be Queen, a town with a Dickens scent about it, a town of the past but healthy, undecayed and prospering in its anachronism.

The run to Stratford was delicious through (I think) the Arden country. Worcester orchards everywhere, purple plums to be picked up at the wayside and apples peeking red-cheeked from innumerable green trees. Woods too on all sides with thick full foliage, and level meadows, and black and white oak-beamed cottages, beyond computation.

Noteworthy was the frequency of the bicycle, especially among road labourers. A group working with a steam-roller had half a dozen laid beside them in the grass with their coats thrown over them. And in the evening, aged labourers, rheumaticky, bent, snow-whiskered, pedalled their tricycles ploddingly homewards from the farm.

Stratford-on-Avon was, in a measure, a disappointment. Shakespeare's day has been almost eliminated. The town is modern and bustling with tourist trafficking. Half a dozen of the ancient houses have been preserved but they stand in streets all built up as fresh as a new century can make them. There is no repose, no contemplation. To gain an insight into the poetry by a visit to the scenes of a poet's life is vain.

The whole district has changed and though still the church of his burial stands by the beautiful Avon, among its ancient headstones, its noble trees, its placid walk by the banks of the stream, the tout stands at its gate, the toll collector awaits within its porch, trippers chatter in its precincts, motor launches flounce about its riverside; only by athletics of the imagination can a dim vision of a sweet grave calm 17th century be conceived by the devout. Yes, one can faintly create the figure of that greatest of men, faintly see him pottering about the lazy village, for it could be little more, lounging in the scented lanes, strolling by the river, chatting to his friend who settled only a few doors from him, amused by the schoolboys' clatter of games and singsong of lessons in the grammar school near by where he too had spent youthful years, listening to country gossip and farmyard profundities, careless of fame or loud repute, at peace after strenuous manhood. Then a motorcycle thuds by, boys wail newspaper cries, the vision mockingly departs. One strolls along to see Marie Corelli's house as a consolation.

I had the magnificent honour of seeing her, a little red-faced yellow-haired podgy woman in expensive white, entering her motor. Well a living dog is better than a dead lion (perhaps!).

The road to Warwick was delightful. The town itself was delicious. Everything about it pleasant and suitable, a much more real artistic treat than Stratford. Gateways, narrow streets, ancient houses, placid river, view of castle, winding lanes with houses whose upper storeys overhung the pavement. Very happy here. On through Kenilworth (a modern town, chiefly a residential suburb of Coventry) by delightful highway to Coventry (61 miles), passing 'Peeping Tom' at the entrance to the town.

Wednesday:
Spent a pleasant evening strolling through streets of Coventry. They were crowded, for the town is a busy industrial centre, which has grown rapidly of recent years. New houses had not yet jostled out the ancient oak-beamed cottages that lurked up narrow entries and cobbled lanes in the dim lamplight. The hotel

I stayed in was an antiquity, my room was a garret, with shaky floors and a view over chimney pots; every chamber was entered by a descending step; the stair climbed steeply upwards precipice fashion, while everything about the house was decayed, the linoleum, the wallpaper, the beds, the tablecloths (especially the tablecloths) and by no means least conspicuously the smell of cooking.

In the morning rain was dripping relentlessly but I set out calmly for Birmingham. My cape protected me and travelling was pleasant. My tyres spurted quietly through the puddles of the soaked road as the rain drizzled silently over the rich green fields and trees around.

Here one passed a big house with its green paddock and broad lawns, there a local builder's, a litter of yellow planks piled together with empty barrels and ladders and trestles. Here a cock crowed cheerily from a farm, or birds chit-chattered from the hedges. Always the tyres spurting in the puddles kept a companionable muttering to compensate for the loneliness. A placid agreeable vegetating journey.

Birmingham a busy but prepossessing city, less dirty than Manchester, with many fine buildings. I took a train here to Leeds (after an 18 mile run) and arrived at 3.15. A young lady from Stoke (her father was an earthenware manufacturer there, she said) made friends with me and I found myself compelled to treat her to tea while she waited for a connection for Hull. I saw her off and set out for Wetherby about 4.20. I saw Leeds in a better light than on my former visit on a walking tour and was impressed very much more favourably than before. Roundhay Park with its lakes and boating seemed a charming spot. The road to Wetherby soon went by and I passed on to Boroughbridge, a delightful clean old-fashioned Yorkshire market town. I met a young fellow in my lodgings who had been in Rouen district cycle-camping at outbreak of war. He had fled to St Malo with refugees and by good luck escaped to Britain with his friends. He had cycled up from Southampton, doing 100 miles a day. He left for the north after tea.

I strolled around the town with much pleasure in the gloaming and the dark, lighted windows gleaming, shadows passing, footsteps clattering on cobbles. An enticing clean bare old town, with none of the decaying picturesqueness of so much of the south. A town of winter winds and storm swept streets, healthy, independent, sturdy. I sat a while in a little public house back parlour, listening to broad Yorkshire tongues, a great treat. Impossible to reproduce the talk but noticeably there was a vigour and individuality and force about the accents and opinions not readily discovered in the southern talk. There was humour in it too, dry, hearty fun of Scottish sort, the southman has weakly ideas of wit. And the faces were jovial and strong, men's faces. And there was no servility. Men met as equals. It was good company.

There was a menagerie in the village – a group of caravans drawn up in three sides of a square with a canopy spread over to form a big tent, in the front an imposing piece of scene painting with an arched entrance, a platform for the band, and a dozen steps, all lit up with arc lamps whose power was generated by a traction engine gay with polished brass and showy decorations.

People were crowding in and the scene was picturesque in the glare that burst out against the black darkness. A shower came down and I hastened away.

Thursday:
This was a big day of mingled pleasure and regret. An early start gave me the joy of the morning sun and breeze on the spreading acres of Yorkshire. The old Roman Road, the Great North Road, rolled almost undeviating over the long miles, the tall telegraph poles merging in distant perspective into the semblance of a huge fence. Long fields stretched in dark or lighter green or vivid yellow stripes between the hedges. Along the wayside flared vivid weed flowers, yellow dandelions, white daisies, purple clover and thistles, scarlet poppies, blue cornflowers, with many others of whose names I am, alas, ignorant.

At intervals, old hostelries, relics of coaching prosperity, faced on the once thronging road, their closed stable buildings and grass grown yards witnessing to the activities of former years. Some bore still the signboards of their trade, others had been transformed to farmhouses without quite losing the appearance of old associations.

Catterick (22 miles) with its wide street, its open spaces before the hotels, its general air of breeziness and elbowroom, looked a typical coaching town; one listened for the post-horns and the clatter of hooves. The old clock chimed the quarters sleepily. Only motors sped through and the inns were deserted.

The run into Darlington (13 miles) was pleasant and the town was prepossessingly clean from that entrance. Hot and blazing was the weather as an August day could be, a sky almost cloudless, a subdued breeze.

The exit had led me through a less pleasant side, a more dirty and grubby aspect of Darlington and the road into Durham was disappointing. Coal mines poured their smoke into the air, now on this side, now on that, spoiling the prospect of the well-farmed countryside. The road was full of steep ascents with little satisfaction in going down their other side. I was tired on entering Durham. Still the cathedral was a compensation. Viewed from every side it was impressive, especially as it rose from the river on a wooded cliff and towered into the sky.

Inside it was extremely simple with Norman pillars of the heaviest type of solidity, some fine glass windows, some beautiful arches, truly one of those poems in architecture that are our most precious heirloom from the past and whose like we too rarely attempt to emulate in these cheap-jack days. Grandeur and grace in stone, how they strike the chord of emotional appreciation! Strange that the effect of music should be achieved by solid masonry! May the traditions of architectural expression be born again in our civilisation so that our aspirations and ideals may be perpetuated even as those of forgotten Normans and Saxons who builded so nobly in the beginning of our history.

After tea I set off for Newcastle. It was a dull road with a vile surface. I was glad to arrive. The bridge over the Tyne had a guard of soldiers and a sentry with fixed bayonet. The city is bristling with soldiers, guarding the Tyne no doubt. Newcastle seems quite a fine city with some worthy buildings and good streets though it is incredibly noisy below my window with newsboys, motor horns, tram bells and general traffic. As my log for the day is 67 miles, I pray for repose.

Friday:

I was wakened by soldiers marching into the station opposite singing 'It's a long way to Tipperary' in the early morning, but I soon slid back again to bed and slept on till seven. I wasted no time in getting out of the hotel for my back tyre was punctured and I wished to find a repair shop. I was fortunate enough to find one soon. Here I had a long chat with a Northumberland man who had been 10 years in Canada without losing his burr. He told me of his experiences with the construction gang of the CPR (Canadian Pacific Railway) and his life on ranches and in cities. I must say the burden of his refrain was of the varied examples of food and catering his travels had afforded him. The picturesque seemed less important than the commissariat to him. He had tried to settle down at home but, hankering after the rough life of freedom, was planning to return next spring.

Passing the large park known as the Town Moor, I saw many hundreds of recruits being drilled with great industry and activity. They marched, counter marched, doubled, halted and marched again in more or less awkward squads, while the brazen voices of drill sergeants rang clamorously over the field. It was amusing to see them collapse on the grass at the readiest opportunity and relax their wearied limbs and backs. And it was evident how much training they would need to become fitted for active service against a continental army.

For a time I watched cavalry manoeuvring in more spectacular fashion. To see a troop disappear slowly into the distance on their heterogeneous mounts was distinctly bizarre. They enabled the imagination to grasp the significance of real warfare conditions. They gave the impression of an outpost troop, scouting perhaps. Talking together, they jogged quietly past on grey ponies, on black horses, on roans and chestnuts of all sizes, rising and falling in their saddles and grouped, for a few moments, before going from sight, in a jumbled mass silhouetted in rough outline. Easy to understand the trepidation of the non-combatant seeing the enemies of his country, sinister and dangerous. Stripped of gay and theatrical trappings, equipped in the harsh uniform of modern war, they presented a menacing impression of ruthless force inspiring dread.

I rode to Morpeth very quietly and then had lunch, afterwards taking a climbing road to Alnwick. There were glorious views of moorland scenery, of wide windy stretches, heather grown and wooded, of a distant hazy sea beside which a white lighthouse gleamed in the sun, of uplands that seemed the roof of England.

The great sweep of the moor would rise against the sky like land against the sea, it looked like the edge of the earth, as though to pass over the ridge would be to topple into space, so abrupt was the line. There was no distance, and over the close horizon the gaze fell only on clouds. A wild country of glorious colours. To pass here in autumn glory would be a delight.

Alnwick was entered through a stout stone portal, for the ancient fortifications that protected this adjunct to the castle of Northumberland's Duke are well preserved. Several gateways still stand over the entries to the little town and the castle guards behind it, anachronisms now in these days of explosive besieging, but interesting and picturesque.

I got four miles on the way to Wooler when I was punctured and there was nothing for it but to attend to the damage at once. I carried the machine down to a river's brink and stripped off the tyre to an accompaniment of grieved profanity. After difficult searching the hole appeared and I took out my solution tube to mend it. The tube had gone dry. I was helpless. Loud and long arose my recrimination to heaven. Further progress was hopeless. I took the four miles back, rather than the 13 miles forward and, after re-inflating the tube six or eight times, plodded back into Alnwick in a shameful retreat. The misfortune was not serious. I reconciled myself to staying overnight in the pleasant little town, and I spent the evening strolling up and down the lively main street, listening to the strains of a patriotic town band ensconced in the room above the gateway, beneath which I had entered for the first time.

Saturday:
I was up betimes. I breakfasted, took my bicycle from the repairers', packed up and caught a half past train for Wooler, being unwilling to lose the time spent through my puncture. The journey over the moorland was full of glorious scenery and I did not regret it. Rain was falling as I left Wooler and I cycled for an hour in a downpour, making for Coldstream. I had just passed

Flodden Field, that spot of ill-omen for a Scotsman, when I discovered another puncture. But I had scarcely time to feel the distress of the affliction when at a blacksmith's door I sighted in passing a cycle wheel and my presence of mind served me sufficiently to ask in an inspiration if they repaired cycles there. In a trice, my machine was being attended to by a smart and tidy apprentice. After the shortest of delays I was spinning securely off again.

I crossed the Tweed into Scotland with a thrill of joy. I felt at home again! The view here was full of dignity and a grave beauty. Scotland prepares a worthy reception for the traveller, entering her gate. The calm Tweed flows beneath a fine bridge, past trees and fields, the village of Coldstream overhanging the banks.

I cycled to Kelso under a clearing sky and left the rain behind as I sped by the winding Tweed. Now and then a view of some old castle uprose by the wayside reminding of the warring days of early history; with often a pretentious modern mansion neighbouring it across the river, the home probably of the present day heir of the old family, and offering in the contrast of opulent luxury with rugged crudity, a striking lesson in history and change of social conditions.

From Kelso I rode to St Boswell's (neglecting Dryburgh Abbey and Abbotsford, both off the main road) to Melrose, where I visited the abbey, a red sandstone ruin much carved and once, no doubt, of considerable dignity. Thence I strove over a steep hill to Galashiels, then through a long pass to Innerleithen and at last to Peebles (60 miles).

The scenery of this run was, perhaps, the most magnificent of the whole fortnight. What countless hills. What glorious fields and valleys. What colour and variety. And what beauty of the gleaming winding Tweed with its reflections and placid calm and peace. It was a fitting termination to a glorious tour and I took the train home, full of a deep satisfaction and content with a well spent holiday, such as I have never had before.

16-28 April 2009

Travel 2

Italy 2009

R D Kernohan

Saturday 25 April

I still hate Heathrow but have one good word for Terminal 5. 'Flight connections' signs often mean short-cuts to long queues but this one spares us a second security search when changing planes.

While we await luggage at Fiumicino my companions exchange tales of theft and peril in Rome, even pockets picked and handbags seized before leaving the airport. But this is one of Italy's many public holidays and thieves are at leisure. We reach our hotel near the Tiber unscathed, even by Roman drivers.

The Casa Valdese is a hotel run by a Protestant company for 'religious and cultural exchanges' and has a Germanic flavour, even what seems a portrait of Goethe in our dining-room. It was once a Roman base for Kaiserswerth deaconesses before being handed over to Italian Protestants and pasta-cooks.

Sunday 26 April

My conscience troubles me only mildly about missing the Scots church on the other side of Rome. Our party are mainly Scottish supporters of the Waldensian Church, topped up with Edinburgh enthusiasts for Italian language and culture, and we pay a fraternal visit to the Protestant church on the Piazza Cavour.

We are rewarded with familiar hymn and psalm-tunes and a lucid and skilful sermon on the Good Shepherd knowing his sheep. (I know it is lucid and skilful, not because I understood most of its melodious flow but because I got an extended summary in Italian, which is easier to read at leisure than follow at length.) The welcoming congregation is sparser than the big church was designed for. The Waldensians have the old Scots passion for a highly educated ministry and intellectually satisfying sermons, with a fine theological college almost next door to the church. But the two growth areas of Italy's Protestant minority want rather different fare. One is among African immigrants. The other, rather larger, is Pentecostal and sets more store on inspiration than higher education.

Monday 27 April

The queue to get into St Peter's looked more daunting than it was, winding along the colonnades and across the square. It took 35 minutes to get in. But the main problem, a sad sign of the times, was delay in getting through airport-style security.

Two of the clichés about St Peter's are quite true. It is so well proportioned that the visitor ceases to notice its enormous size. It is also so vast that great crowds are easily dispersed inside, with minor congestion only at St Peter's statue. Being more of a traditional than hygienic cast of mind, I was sorry to see that the customary procedure now seems to be to lay a hand on Peter's big toe rather than kiss it. But as I intended neither I couldn't complain.

Being a royalist, although a very Hanoverian one, I sought out the Stuart memorial. But it was less to sigh over that dynasty than to remember a very good Scottish journalist, Ion S Munro, who was still contributing to the Herald in my time, long after his days as Rome correspondent of the Morning Post, and writing books on Mussolini's Italy. While in Rome he built up a rare collection of Jacobite books and memorabilia which he had stowed away in an Islington square but meant to leave to Stirling University. I hope they got there.

We have had one or two unhappy experiences over meals (including a real rip-off down the street from the Vatican) and for dinner carefully chose a restaurant with Italians in it. But when we tell the waiter that we are Britannici, but Scozzesi and not Inglesi, he professes a devotion to the heroic William Wallace. Later we realise he has probably seen *Braveheart*.

Prices are reasonable, and but for sterling's weakness would seem moderate for a capital. However my reflections on comparative prices get me into a fankle about the tip. Outside I tell my wife I have under-tipped Wallace (which I probably hadn't) and she tells me to go back and give him more, which really makes his day.

Tuesday 28 April

Walked in the rain (even a delicious Roman spring has wet days) to the Vatican museums. People have to see them but I'm not sure how much they appreciate them. At 18 Euros a head, counting booking-fee, to escape the long queue, they're expensive. You pay for the lot even if you only want to see one or two, even just the Sistine Chapel.

I suppose the chapel would be insufferably overcrowded if admission were in any other way. As it is, it's never a haven of peace but I found more scope for contemplation than I expected by getting a seat and gazing at Michelangelo's *Last Judgment* and the ceiling.

The easiest way to get value for admission is probably to take time to look at picture collections in the Borgia apartments (which include a Graham Sutherland and Francis Bacon as 'modern religious art') and in the Pinacoteca back near the entrance. It includes great Italian religious art but one or two incongruities. The gallery has long seen the departing visitor out with the Lawrence portrait of George IV, which its subject presented to the Pope, but someone has also slipped in a small picture of Voltaire.

Some items may also be in tactful storage. That robust Scottish novelist and traveller, Tobias Smollett, always eager to be affronted, made much of a couple of Vatican 'religious' pictures revelling in the atrocities of the St Bartholomew's Day massacre of Huguenots, but I found no such breaches of the ecumenical peace. I even picked up on audio-guide a good dissertation on the role of religious art in inter-faith dialogue. But I wondered what Japanese tourist parties made of pictures and frescos that demand more than nodding acquaintances with both the Old Testament and the Gospels.

Back for dinner to Wallace's restaurant. He is looking forward to a lucrative evening and lays on the treatment – corner table, devoted attention to the signora, no charge for little extras, house wine served with a flourish fit for a rarer vintage. The food is good too. But he traps me at the end because I am almost out of small notes and coins and pay with a large one. The change comes in minor coin and one still quite big note. I either have to give it to him or insult him with a trifle. He wins.

Wednesday 29 April

If Roman museums can be extravagantly dear, Roman churches are free and dozens are worth seeing. This morning we paid the inevitable visit to the Colosseum and Forum but started off with San Pietro in Vincoli nearby, notable for Michelangelo's statue of Moses on a papal tomb. On the way we passed through a little enclave of Africa, for not all the immigrants who slip across the Mediterranean head for Calais and Dover.

Having seen a papal tomb, we got to the fringe of a papal audience by mistake. The bus from the Colosseum was a travelling sardine tin, so packed that we gasped off at the Piazza Venezia (where Mussolini once held forth) and decided to take the first reasonably empty bus wherever it was going. It headed for the Castel Sant'Angelo but got held up at St Peter's Square, full of seats on which some invited audience was watching the Pope on giant TV screens.

Later I took time to look at the papers. On the Metro there were copies of a free tabloid Metro but no-one will manage to read it on Roman buses. The broadsheets are good, though taken over by swine flu and Berlusconi's domestic troubles. But the best, the Corriere della Sera and La Stampa, remain based in Milan and Turin, not Rome.

Thursday 30 April

The Roman Metro has some forbiddingly sepulchral stations and shabby vandalised coaches on Line B, but the smarter Line A takes us straight to St John's Lateran. The approach is made hideous by what seems a test-run for an open-air pop concert. The din intrudes into the church except at the far end where it gives way to what Browning called 'the blessed mutter of the Mass'.

Across the road is the Scala Santa, which many pious visitors climb on their knees. Judging by the souvenir stalls outside, half of them must be Polish. The steps are well filled, not just with older pilgrims but with some earnest young people and a few bewildered-looking children. I find the guidance for visitors and, reading between the lines, conclude that the author is no more convinced than I am that this is Pontius Pilate's staircase. The holiness, it suggests, comes from the devotion associated with the site. But when I get to the last paragraph I am told that if I sincerely repent of my sins, I can get an indulgence, and presumably time off in Purgatory, even if I spare my knees and nip up the side staircases. I am not pleased, for I agree with Dr Luther on these matters.

We eat again at William Wallace's. This time I mean to go easy on tipping. But it's his night off and we get a pretty waitress, so no economy is possible. I also discover the hard way that salmon tagliatelli in Rome are not what they are in Scottish-Italian restaurants. They come soaked in what supermarkets sell as 'sea-food sauce'.

Friday 1 May
It's another public holiday and no-one is up but tourists. We stroll to the Piazza del Popolo which I remember as beautiful but has been made ugly by traffic-planning and structures for some special event. That hastens us on our way through old Rome and past the Parliament to the Pantheon, which is where I recommend newcomers to Rome start their pilgrimage. For this, more than the magnificence of St Peter's, shows the history, continuity, and diversity of Rome. The Roman temple, a graceful triumph of civil engineering, survived virtually unchanged as a church, and the tombs of Raphael and the first kings of united Italy are an introduction to both an artistic heritage and a troubled history.

Somewhere nearby we find a touring-bus stop. It's an expensively pleasant trip, with two limitations. Most of the audio-points are out of order so that we cannot hear the commentary, and the itinerary in no way resembles the one on the tour-map. I worry about a possible mystery tour down the Appian Way when we ought to be thinking about transport to the airport. My wife concurs rather than agrees when after passing Santa Maria Maggiore yet again I insist on catching the Metro to get back for our luggage. But the trip was worthwhile. We were stuck for a bit beside a plaque commemorating Margaret Fuller, of whom I hadn't heard. It turns out she was a feminist, journalist, and the first woman war correspondent, back in Garibaldi's time.

On the internet, and from various sources, I was assured of a fixed rate of 40 Euros for taxis to the airport. The taxi driver does not share this view but we reach a concordat, rather weighted in his favour. I suppose the Romans have been fleecing tourists for over 2,000 years and are not likely to change now.

But I give thanks where due. This time my wife didn't want a drive on a Roman buggy (where previous experience suggests you get a placid horse and excitably importunate driver). Nor was there was any suggestion that we throw coins in fountains. Given the Euro exchange rate, that was just as well.

14 May 2009

Part X

Rear window

Rear window 1

Graveyard of the rich

Barbara Millar

The view from my Glasgow hotel room was peaceful. As it should have been – it was overlooking the Ramshorn kirkyard. The flat grave slabs were lightly dusted with snow. Crocuses were just beginning to peek their purple heads around the forbidding iron 'cages', designed to thwart the grave-robbing 'Resurrectionists'. All was still, tranquil.

The kirkyard – Glasgow's oldest – is, along with the church crypt, the last resting place of some of the city's most celebrated sons. Located in the heart of the once thriving and prosperous Merchant City, the wealthy and their families were happy to pay more to be buried in 'Paradise'. Reading the inscriptions provides a fascinating snapshot of an 18th-century Glasgow elite – millionaires and misers, philanthropists and misanthropes, those at the cutting edge of the day's technology – and, naturally, bankers. But as well as holding the dust of various luminaries, it also protects secrets.

In the Fleming family lair, but without anything to signify his occupation of it, is Pierre Emile L'Angelier, a 33-year-old from Jersey, whose name, perhaps, is significantly less familiar than that of his scheming lover, Madeleine Smith. Pierre died of arsenic poison, after consuming a cup of cocoa (the third, the previous two made him ill but still he went back for more) delivered through Madeleine's Blythswood Square bedroom window, a seemingly thoughtful gesture on a cold night, but one designed to end Pierre's threats to expose Madeleine's lack of virtue to her strict father, after she ended their liaison when another beau made a better marriage offer.

He died in agony and Madeleine's subsequent nine-day trial hit the headlines – as did the sensational verdict of 'not proven'. Madeleine went on to live to the grand age of 92. Pierre went to the Ramshorn kirkyard. It is likely that the true story of her hand in that pitiful death may never be revealed.

Perhaps the most celebrated of the Glasgow 'tobacco lords', John Glassford, described by novelist Tobias Smollett as 'one of the greatest merchants in Europe', is a neighbour. The flamboyant, ambitious Glassford started trading in tobacco in 1750 when he was 35 years old, and quickly built up an enormous fleet of 25 ships to ply the lucrative trade across the Atlantic. He ran tobacco stores along the east coast of north America and some £1/2m passed through his hands – a formidable amount of money at that time. He had a country house out at Milngavie and a town house, the Shawfield Mansion, on the corner of Trongate and what is now, appropriately, Glassford Street.

He also had interests in a stocking manufacturing company, a dyeing and printing works, a tannery and a couple of banks, the Glasgow Arms and the Thistle. But he was a hopeless gambler – literally – and died with enormous debts. Quite unlike another kirkyard occupant, millionaire banker Robert Carrick, who started out as a junior clerk in the Ship Bank and ended up as its manager and a partner. He lived, frugally, above the shop, although he also had a country mansion at Mount Vernon. But, despite amassing a fortune of over £1m, he had a deserved reputation as a miser, and died 'a grim old bachelor, without leaving one plack or one penny to any of the charitable institutions of the city'.

This is in marked contrast to John Anderson, known to his students at Glasgow University – where he was professor of natural philosophy, with a special enthusiasm for physics – as 'Jolly Jack Phosphorus', because of his love of experiments, especially if they involved fireworks and explosions. Friend of James Watt, Anderson was a liberal educator, who wanted to provide 'useful learning' for working-class people. He offered non-academic evening lectures, open to men and women, and, when he died, bequeathed a large amount of money to found Anderson's Institution – today evolved as Strathclyde University.

A public servant who was responsible for clearing and landscaping Glasgow Green, to create a public park, also resides at the Ramshorn. James Cleland was superintendent of public works and later wrote *The Annals of Glasgow*, providing a history of the city's public services, societies and institutions, although it was published many years later than the books produced by the Foulis brothers, Robert and Andrew, who were once within the kirkyard but are now deep under the tarmac of Ingram Street, victims of the road widening in the 1820s, and now remembered by a plaque with their initials.

The Foulis brothers were Glasgow University's printers and were recognised for producing very accurate editions of Latin and Greek classical works. Intent on publishing a totally accurate version of Horace, they employed six highly experienced proof-readers but, even so, their final 'immaculate' version came out with six misprints. In 1753, they founded an academy of art in Glasgow – Scotland's first – where pupils learned the techniques of drawing, engraving, painting and sculpture.

Entrepreneur David Dale, who established the New Lanark cotton mills on the banks of the River Clyde, rests within the Ramshorn confines. Exceptionally for his time, Dale provided education and care for his workers, an approach extended by his son-in-law, Robert Owen, to whom Dale sold the mills. He provided financial assistance to the new Royal Infirmary and was a director of the city's poorhouse. His father-in-law was a director of the Royal Bank of Scotland in Edinburgh and Dale opened the first RBS branch in Glasgow. I looked closely, but – surprisingly – could see no sign of the ground having been disturbed by rapid body-revolving movements below.

But certainly the strangest thing to have been interred in the Ramshorn kirkyard is a single leg. The leg was found in the garden of a house in Candleriggs and the owner of the house consulted the Ramshorn minister about what to do. Eventually, the leg was laid to rest – without ceremony, without stone, without inscription, because, the minister insisted, he could not be sure it was a Christian leg.

26 March 2009

Rear window 2

1320: a Scottish myth?

Andrew Hook

Currently Scotland boasts four United Nations-designated world heritage sites: Edinburgh, St Kilda, New Lanark, and neolithic Orkney. Over the last four years, however, a campaign has been underway to have Arbroath Abbey added to the list of Scottish sites winning such international recognition. In normal circumstances, a campaign of this kind would be based on the importance and architectural beauty of the abbey ruins, but in this instance such is not the case. Instead the campaign argues it is the abbey's connection with the Declaration of Arbroath that makes it worthy of world heritage status. As Mike Weir, the SNP MP for Angus puts it: 'The influence of the events that took place at Arbroath on 6 April 1320, and the words of that declaration, is a global one. Democracies around the world can find their founding principles in the Declaration of Arbroath. It is only right that Arbroath Abbey has the opportunity to win full international recognition as a world heritage site.'

The idea that the 1320 Declaration of Arbroath (most historians are less confident than Mike Weir appears to be that it can be precisely dated to 6 April) can be seen as providing a template for the emergence of democracy worldwide is backed up by one, outstanding example: the 1776 American Declaration of Independence. Ever since Trent Lott persuaded the Senate of the United States in 1998 to nominate 6 April as America's national tartan day, a relationship between the two declarations has been accepted as an historical fact. The 1998 Senate resolution flatly asserts that there is a crucial link between Scotland and the US going back to 1320: the Declaration of Independence was modelled, it states, on the Declaration of Arbroath. Given this as it were official ratification, it is hardly surprising that politicians, commentators, leader writers, and journalists everywhere – but particularly within Scotland – go on accepting this relationship as historically accurate.

Repetition of an idea, however, does not amount to evidence of its accuracy. And when one asks, quite simply, what exactly is the evidence that the framers of the American Declaration of Independence in Philadelphia in 1776 had the Arbroath Declaration in mind when drawing up their document, nothing specific emerges. Thomas Jefferson is known to have been the principal author of the American document. Does Jefferson cite the Declaration of Arbroath? No. Had Jefferson read the Arbroath declaration? Did he even know of its existence? There is no hard evidence in favour of a positive answer to either question. Of course there were two native-born Scots involved in the debates over the wording of the American document – John Witherspoon, a Presbyterian clergyman and president of the College of New Jersey in Princeton, and James Wilson, a lawyer in Philadelphia – and they would become the only Scottish signers of the final version of the Declaration of Independence. Products of the Scottish universities system, it is perhaps possible that they were at least aware of the letter that the Scottish barons addressed to the Pope in 1320. But they make no mention of it in their writings.

In his 2003 book *For Freedom Alone: The Declaration of Arbroath 1320*, my good friend, Ted Cowan, professor of Scottish history at Glasgow University, does his very best in a concluding chapter to make the case for the influence of the Scottish declaration on the American one. But I think he would agree that he finds nothing in the way of conclusive evidence. Possibilities, likelihoods, yes – but hard evidence? No. Meanwhile David Armitage, professor of history at Harvard University, and author of *The Declaration of Independence: A Global History* sees no link between the two documents. In the course of research for my own book *Scotland and America 1750-1835*, I read widely in American journals and magazines in the later 18th century. I found manifold references to Scottish books and writers; to Scottish philosophy and education; to Scottish history and science. All the leading figures in both the Scottish Enlightenment and Scottish literary romanticism were well-known in America. But references to Arbroath? Not one.

My own view is in fact the reverse of the current orthodoxy. It was the Declaration of Independence that influenced Arbroath.

My point is that the 1320 letter insisting on the freedom and independence of the Scottish people, and asking the Pope to recognise the legitimacy of Robert the Bruce's claim to the Scottish throne, only began to be called the Declaration of Arbroath some time in the 20th century. In the brilliant 11th edition of the *Encyclopaedia Britannica*, for example, the entry on Arbroath includes reference to the 1320 letter but the phrase 'Declaration of Arbroath' does not appear. The chances then are quite high that the letter from the Scottish nobility became known as the Declaration of Arbroath because of the universal popularity of America's Declaration of Independence.

The even greater irony is that the focus on Arbroath has prevented general recognition that Scotland did indeed make a major contribution to the creation of the Declaration of Independence – not through the romance of its medieval past, but through the Scottish Enlightenment and the learning of several of its 18th-century philosophers, including Francis Hutcheson, David Hume, and Lord Kames.

5 May 2009

Rear window 3

Reading the Riot Act

Barbara Millar

The weekend newspapers have been full of it. The wave of wildcat strikes at oil refineries, power stations and chemical plants across Britain – with other workers due to discuss taking their own imminent industrial action – has been dubbed 'the dawn of a new age of unrest'.

It has been a long time since strikes hit the headlines. So there was a certain sad piquancy that this action coincided, almost to the day, with the anniversary of one of the bloodiest occurrences in labour history – the battle of George Square in Glasgow on Friday 31 January 1919, a day which also saw the last reading of the Riot Act. The Scottish Trades Union Council and the Clyde Workers Committee (CWC) called a '40-hour strike' in January 1919 to demand a reduction in working hours. The immediate objective in reducing the hours was to stimulate the creation of thousands of jobs for the troops coming home after the end of the First World War.

Before the war, the working week had been 54 hours and, while Scottish workers wanted to see it cut to 30, Emanuel (Manny) Shinwell, then the Glasgow Trades Council president, persuaded them to go for a more realistic 40-hour week. On 29 January 1919, after a rally of strikers in Glasgow and a march to George Square, a deputation from the CWC – headed by Shinwell – managed to secure a meeting with the Lord Provost, Sir James Watson Stuart. At this meeting, strike leaders requested that the Lord Provost ask the government to compel employers to grant workers a 40-hour week. The Lord Provost asked the strike leaders to return on 31 January when he assured them he would give a reply.

On Friday 31 January more than 60,000 people descended on George Square to hear the Lord Provost deliver the government's response to their 40-hour demand. The strike leaders went into the City Chambers for the meeting. What happened next – the precise cause of the riot – has long been bitterly disputed, with some saying it was caused by an unprovoked baton charge by the City of Glasgow police, while others contend it was set off by strikers, trying to prevent trams running through the square.

In his book *Revolt on the Clyde*, Willie Gallacher, who was one of the strike leaders present, says: 'Suddenly, without warning of any kind, a signal was given and the police made a savage and totally unexpected assault on the rear of the meeting, smashing right and left with their batons, utterly regardless of whom or what they hit.' In response, the crowd hit back with fists and feet, tore up railings and used broken bottles from a lemonade lorry as weapons. Fighting went on throughout the night and 53 people – 34 strikers, 19 policemen – were injured by the end of hostilities. A pamphlet by revolutionary socialist John Maclean, one of the Red Clydesiders, laid the blame firmly on police chief constable James Stevenson and James Dalrymple, general manager of Glasgow tramways, whom he accused of intimidating tram drivers to ensure trams were driven through George Square on the day of the protest.

Although some of the tram drivers had joined the strike, most had not and, according to Maclean, this had the desired effect of pitting the blackleg tram drivers against the strikers. Stevenson, argued Maclean, employed traffic regulations which were designed to irritate the demonstrators and provoke violence between them and the police.

During the riot, the sheriff started to read the Riot Act. It was snatched from his hands. This act had been introduced 200 years earlier, in 1714, in order to allow local authorities to be able to declare any group of more than a dozen people to be unlawfully assembled, and thus have to disperse or face punishment. It was first used after the Sacheverell riots of 1715, when Henry Sacheverell, a high church preacher, used the 21st anniversary of the 1688 'Glorious Revolution' to cast doubts on its legitimacy.

The act, whose long title was: 'An act for preventing tumults and riotous assemblies and for the more speedy and effectual punishment of the rioters' was used throughout its history for the maintenance of civil order and for political means. If groups failed to disperse within an hour, then anyone remaining gathered was guilty of a felony, punishable by death, and anyone assisting with the dispersal was specifically indemnified against any legal consequences in the event of any of the crowd being injured or killed.

After the Riot Act was read in George Square, strike leaders Manny Shinwell and Willie Gallacher were arrested, charged with incitement to riot and imprisoned for five months and three months respectively. In the days and weeks that followed Glasgow resembled an armed camp. The government sent in 10,000 troops largely from England (no Scottish troops from the nearby Maryhill barracks were deployed) and, according to one eyewitness account: 'The whole city bristled with tanks and machine guns'.

On 10 February 1919, the 40-hour strike was called off by the strike leaders and the striking workers from the engineering and shipbuilding industries returned to their jobs, having negotiated a 47-hour working week, 10 hours fewer than they were working before the strike. Whatever the outcome of the current industrial unrest, one thing is for sure – the Riot Act can never be read again. The outdated legislation was finally repealed in 1973 (by which time, of course, riot was no longer punishable by death). Ninety years ago, on 'Black Friday', in Glasgow's George Square, was the last time its words were ever heard.

3 February 2009

Rear window 4

Naked Edinburgh

Andrew Hook

Last Sunday's coverage of the Edinburgh Festival in the Observer included this comment on the international book festival: 'While every other festival venue is on a crazy Darwinian mission to expand, reinvent, colonise, the book fest stays politely as it should, a civilised little blue and green planet parked in Charlotte Square'.

This image of the book festival as a centre of decorous calm surrounded by the publicity-seeking alarums and excursions of the rest of the Fringe gave me instant pause. Lifting my coffee cup in a kind of salute, I remembered the different world in which for the first time the Edinburgh International Festival was persuaded to extend its coverage of contemporary arts by venturing into the world of books.

The year was 1962. As the most junior of junior lecturers in Edinburgh University's English department I happened to become involved in the organisation of what became known as the 'Writers' Conference' – an official event in that year's festival programme. The idea of staging such an event had been initially dreamed up by Jim Haynes, that colourful and kenspeckle American who had arrived in Edinburgh a few years earlier, studied briefly at the university, and then bought out a junkshop in Charles Street to establish the first paperback bookshop in Scotland. Not far from George Square, in the area that in subsequent years the university in its wisdom would convert into a shabby wasteland, the shop soon became a focus for everything that was lively and progressive and avant-garde in Edinburgh's cultural life. Jim pursued the idea of a writers' conference with John Calder, the Scottish (but London-based) publisher of Samuel Beckett and other key modernist writers. Calder brought on board Sonia Orwell, widow of George. And Lord Harewood, then the festival director, finally gave his consent.

Everything had to be organised in no time at all. Sonia Orwell was probably the key figure. She seemed to know everyone and the writers she approached seemed always willing to take part. So remarkably the conference duly took place in the McEwan Hall between the 20th and 24th of August 1962. There were sessions on such topics as censorship, the future of the novel, and contemporary Scottish writing.

The line-up of writers was pretty impressive – Norman Mailer, Mary McCarthy, Henry Miller, Lawrence Durrell, Hugh McDiarmid, David Daiches, Angus Wilson, and many more. Inevitably there were some no-shows, but all in all the whole event was regarded as a major success, giving the Edinburgh Festival a whole new dimension. So much so that in the following year Haynes and the others were allowed to organise a Drama Conference. Same location, same style. But this time disaster struck.

On the last day of the conference a theatrical 'happening' was staged in the McEwan Hall. It ended with a naked model being wheeled across the hall's organ loft. Bourgeois Edinburgh was outraged. The city fathers made it clear to the festival's organisers that such morally offensive events would not be tolerated. There would be no more writers' conferences.

Despite his crucial involvement in the creation of the original Traverse Theatre, Jim Haynes would soon leave Edinburgh for London and a wider world. Today of course a naked model on the Fringe would hardly be worth a comment. And the occasional controversies stirred by writers' remarks at the book festival are rarely much more than storms in teacups. Life and letters, I feel, were very different – and perhaps more engaging – in the Edinburgh of the early 60s.

22 August 2008

Part XI

Books of the year

A personal selection by
Scottish Review contributors

Alan Fisher

My favourite book of the year is *Watching the Door* by Kevin Myers. The memoir of a journalist who finds himself in Belfast almost by accident, it perfectly captures the frightening reality and the black humour of the early years of the troubles. He'd like to paint the place as a hellhole, where murders are routinely carried out on street corners in the name of one cause or another but he makes a lively and engaging story out of the sense of evil he feels lies across the city. His Belfast is not the one I recognise from my time in the city but in saying 'The absence of sense is what makes wars possible' he captures much of what was wrong in Northern Ireland for 30 years.

Rose Galt

The serendipitous find was *Mr Pip* by a New Zealand writer hitherto unknown in the UK, Lloyd Jones. Set in the civil war-ridden island of Bougainville in Papua New Guinea, it is a first person account by a young girl, Matilda, of how her life is changed by her attendance, against her mother's wishes, at the village school, run by an eccentric white man and with only one book, Dickens' *Great Expectations*. It was the difficult third in Waterstone's 3-for-2 offer and it simply blew me away.

The second is the Orange Prize winner *The Road Home* by Rose Tremain. Its hero Lev, a grieving widower with a young daughter and a mother to support, takes the horrific 30-hour bus journey from his home in an unnamed eastern European country to London to find work. It is a deeply humane story of exile and loss, fear and hope, and in no way a political diatribe. Tremain has a particular gift for characterisation and the people who inhabit Lev's new life as well as his marvellous pal, Rudi, back home, spring to life from her pages. In less skilled hands they could so easily have become clichéd stereotypes. A truly uplifting novel that nevertheless had me in tears. Don't finish it on the bus.

Sheila Hetherington

If the definition of a favourite book is one that has been greatly enjoyed, and occasionally returned to over many years with renewed interest and pleasure, let me nominate *Kristin*

Lavransdatter by Sigrid Undset. It is a saga set in 14th-century Norway. Kristin, the central character, comes through great tribulation, often as a result of her own impulsive nature, as we travel alongside her (for 1,000 pages), from her childhood to her death in the black plague epidemic. Undset's historical references are impeccable, as is her understanding of human nature, with all its frailties.

My copy of the book – actually three books in one – is the earlier translation by Charles Archer and J C Scott. I understand that a later translation by Tilda Nunnery is recommended.

Andrew Hook

Occasionally I bump into people who once upon a time were students of mine. Perhaps they recall odd lectures I'd given on *King Lear* or *Paradise Lost* or *The Scarlet Letter* or *The Great Gatsby*. But sometimes they remember something else of more permanent benefit: that I'd recommended *The Elements of Style* by Strunk and White. Originally published in 1959, hardly a hundred pages long, and constantly reprinted, it is the one and only guide to good writing I believe in. Keep it at your side.

For me the best of 2008 was *Kieron Smith, Boy*. James Kelman back on top form. A wonderfully imaginative recreation of ordinary Scottish life and culture.

Walter Humes

The book that made the most impact on me during 2008 was Maggie Fergusson's splendid biography of the Orcadian writer George Mackay Brown. I picked it up in a bookshop in Stromness while on a brief visit to Orkney. It captivated me from beginning to end. Not only is it a scrupulously researched study of the man and his work, it is a wonderful evocation of the landscape that inspired so many of Brown's poems and stories. We gain a vivid sense of his struggles – against poverty, depression and ill-health – but also of his courage and creativity in transforming the material of a restricted life into words that express many of the eternal truths of the human condition.

R D Kernohan

When Alexander Solzhenitsyn died I re-read *The Gulag*

Archipelago and *The First Circle*, the most complex of his semi-autobiographical novels. The old power was there, even though he may not translate easily, but my emotional reactions were inevitably more complex. He still commands awe and honour, for this is some of the great historical art of the 20th-century. But what further complexities of human nature are revealed when old KGB men hold power but ostentatiously cross themselves at funerals in restored cathedrals of Holy Russia!

The obituaries made much of these enigmas in the new Russia and Solzhenitsyn's reluctance to endorse liberal democracy, and when they mentioned his rediscovery of Russia's Orthodox faith they presented this as an alienation from the West. They did not make enough of the broad Christian humanism evident in his books and his solidarity in captivity with many sorts of conditions of victims, whether of Stalin's cruelty or Lenin's legacy.

Fiona MacDonald

Bill Bryson's *Shakespeare* was my holiday reading this summer. A vivid account of the bard's life and times, it is both highly entertaining – in the way that Bryson always is – and informative. When I started to read Eric Sykes's autobiography *If I Don't Write It, Nobody Else Will*, I didn't really expect that I would stick with it until the end, but it is a strangely compulsive book – poignant on the subject of his childhood, gossipy and funny.

Barbara Millar

St Monans is a small village just a couple of miles from where I live in the East Neuk of Fife. Once it had a thriving fishing industry. Now it boasts a smart restaurant, a handful of shops and a good line in tourism, being a stop on the magnificent Fife coastal path. Back in the 1940s it was also the childhood home of Christopher Rush, who graphically relates the story of his upbringing in the remarkable autobiography *Hellfire and Herring*.

Mairi Clare Rodgers

Although not new, a book that moved me deeply this year was

Siri Hustvedt's *What I Loved*. A ferociously intelligent book, full of truths about men, women and the gaping chasm in between. Part intellectual lecture, part old-fashioned page turner, *What I Loved* engages, provokes and disturbs. She presents uncomfortable statements that ring true; at one point a character observes that they've 'always thought that love thrives on a certain kind of distance. That it requires an awed separateness to continue. Without that necessary remove, the physical minutiae of the other person grows ugly in its magnification'. An uneasy thought, yet utterly familiar. *What I Loved* is a compelling read which will stay with you long after you have turned the last page.

23 December 2008

Part XII

Religion

Religion 1

Spot the difference

Walter Humes

I see that an atheist advertising campaign has been launched with the slogan 'There's probably no God. Now stop worrying and enjoy your life'. Not exactly snappy but it gets the message across. Over the next month buses will carry the advertisements in Glasgow, Edinburgh, Dundee and Aberdeen, as well as cities in England and Wales. Members of the public have raised funds to finance the campaign, which also received support from the British Humanist Association and the author of *The God Delusion*, Richard Dawkins.

One of the people responsible for the initiative had objected to a series of Christian adverts on London buses and wanted to provide an alternative perspective. That suggests a rather negative motivation, though in a democratic society individuals and groups should certainly have the freedom to challenge beliefs that they regard as misleading or damaging. Moreover, it can be argued that in Western societies Christianity has had a very good innings, dominating thinking and exercising considerable power for many centuries. The Church of England, an institution which I find it difficult to take seriously, still has a significant constitutional role and its bishops are given a platform from which to speak in the House of Lords. It is not difficult to construct a case which suggests that, historically, the institutional church has been an oppressive agency in relation to many groups – women, children, dissenters, homosexuals and other minorities. Equally, however, at an individual level, many Christians over the centuries have demonstrated courage, compassion and selflessness of an exceptional kind.

I write this as a non-believer but as someone who has in the past worked in a Christian (Catholic) institution and who has been enriched by colleagues whose faith has been a vital part of their identity. Although I do not share their beliefs, I can respect their stance and learn from their perspectives on life. A number of them would also wish to draw the distinction between the personal and the institutional dimensions of faith. Many Catholics are now prepared to depart from approved doctrine on particular issues, while retaining their allegiance to what they see as the fundamentals of their church.

The atheists undoubtedly have a right to present their case but I think they need to be careful about the style and tone they adopt. Here a distinction between commitment and zealotry is relevant. There is a difference between, on the one hand, holding a view with conviction and arguing for it strongly and, on the other, having a closed mind to the point where no amount of reasoning, however well-founded, will influence one's thinking. Ironically, there is a danger that atheists might display some of the same characteristics as those they are seeking to counter. Dogmatic atheism would be just as unattractive as dogmatic religion.

Not long ago I watched a television programme in which Richard Dawkins was debating with a Muslim cleric. What struck me at the time was that it was the Muslim cleric who seemed rational and logical in his arguments, while Dawkins came across as authoritarian and fundamentalist. There is a lesson here, similar to the one which draws attention to the fact that the extremes of the political left and the political right have much in common: a rigid, intolerant ideology and a desire to change minds in such a way that nothing will allow the victims to think for themselves. There is a name for this process: it is called indoctrination.

8 January 2009

Religion 2

Cause célèbre

Alex Wood

There's a Presbyterian streak in many Scots, including those without denominational affiliation or even religion, but that serious concern about ethical issues is insufficient to explain the interest in the Scott Rennie case at the General Assembly. It is almost unbelievable, as we approach the second decade of the 21st century, that sexual orientation should be the centre of national debate.

The fundamentalist view, however, is clear and unambiguous. The Bible is the literal word of God. 'Thou shalt not lie with mankind as with womankind; it is an abomination.' (Leviticus 18). A homosexual lifestyle is incompatible with biblical teaching. The Bible says it is an abomination: end of debate, despite the fact that the Bible contains serious contradictions (examine the contradictory promises to the poor in the two versions of the sermon on the mount) and injunctions which few contemporary Christians would uphold – husbands separating from their menstruating wives or the incestuous seduction of their father by Lot's daughters.

Nonetheless the strength of the fundamentalist position should never be doubted. I'm reminded of the daughter of a Free Presbyterian manse who gave her parents a Scotsman calendar, one of the illustrations of which noted mountains which were several millions of years old. When next she visited her parents the calendar was on the wall but 'several million' had been deleted and replaced by '6,000' because the literal interpretation of Genesis is inconsistent with scientific views of the earth's evolutionary timescale.

The opponents of homosexual practice frequently revert to the argument of its being unnatural. The now common placard, 'God created Adam and Eve, not Adam and Steve', sums up a view of the issue otherwise expressed as, 'It's just not right, it's not natural', a highly dangerous argument in the context of sexuality. The common acts of homosexual sex are all practised in heterosexual sex. A few of the puritanical brethren and elders might seek to proscribe explicitly and exactly which sexual behaviours are acceptable and which unacceptable but Iranian-style moral control is unimaginable.

A more telling argument is that if Scott Rennie were heterosexual he would not be permitted by the church to live in an active sexual relationship with a partner to whom he is not married and maintain his ministry. There can't be a more lax rule for the homosexual ministry than for the heterosexual ministry. The impact of accepting Scott Rennie as a minister is that the Kirk must now consider same sex marriage. At one level that should offer few intellectual problems since marriage in Scotland has been viewed since the Reformation, by the Kirk as well as the law, as a civil contract but such a sea-change will not occur quickly.

Perhaps most worrying for the Kirk's liberals is that to legitimise same sex unions undermines the very institution of the family. Marriage may not in reformed tradition be a sacrament, and for the irreligious marriage may merely be a social construct, but many agree that it is the best vehicle to raise children. To state that marriage is the best place within which to raise children does not assume that the procreation of children is its primary purpose. No Protestant church starts today from the expectation that all who marry will wish to have children, nor would any such church refuse, say, to marry a couple one or both of whom were infertile. The family is evolving from what it was and same sex marriage is not what threatens the family as an institution.

Scott Rennie's call to Queen's Cross has whipped up a storm in the Presbyterian tea-cup. The narrowness of the victory of the liberals is indicative of the strength of social conservatism in the Church of Scotland. Perhaps it has grabbed attention because it exposes the narrowness of the liberal consensus; perhaps because it signals another step towards the gradual demise of the Kirk; perhaps because it plays to Scotland's prurient side; perhaps because it facilitated cheap headlines.

The issue will likely be forgotten in a few months but for this writer it had a personal significance. Rennie is presently minister at Brechin Cathedral, where I was baptised and my parents married. Brechin was the birthplace of Thomas Guthrie, founder of the ragged schools movement, campaigner for temperance, a prime mover in the disruption of 1843, leader of a stern, unbending and fundamentalist evangelism. Brechin was, and I thought is, a quiet backwater of social conservatism which I still visit regularly, whose football team I support but which I had never considered as an exemplar of tolerance. Yet Scott Rennie asserts that Brechin has lived amicably with its divorced, gay minister and his partner for several years. If Brechin can rise to that, perhaps this atheist can believe there's some hope for a more tolerant and humane Scotland in the years ahead.

28 May 2009

Religion 3

Thoughts for Christmas

Bruce Gardner

The world can be a dark place, and many people throughout the history of Europe found winter dreadful. For that reason, midwinter festivals were common, a chance to celebrate the promise of spring in what we rightly call the 'dead' of winter. Four days after the winter solstice (or 'shortest day'), it begins to be obvious that the days are lengthening and that they will continue to do so...all the way to spring.

In the Roman case, four days from the solstice on 21 December brought them to Die Sol Invictis, 'Day of the Unconquered Sun', on 25 December. So, when the Roman Empire turned officially 'Christian' in the time of Emperor Constantine, it seemed natural to replace the pagan festival with a suitably popular Christian one. From such humble beginnings was our Christmas born. So, while *In the bleak midwinter* is sincere, it is a bit fanciful: there may have been no wintry scene, with snow, when Christ was born – whenever that was.

There are three things to say about this: to begin with, the 'pagan' festival came first, with feasting, drinking, log fires and sharing of presents. Fine sermons on 'getting back to what Christmas is all about' may thus be sincere, but uninformed. A cracking good conversation around an open fire is a bit older than singing carols.

Secondly, those who object to Christmas having 'a pagan past' are also fairly naive. There is nothing devilish in wanting to warm your hands at the fireside and share a party with friends. I also note that those who object to Christmas as a festival and profess to be too holy to get involved in it, while they may also call Sunday the Sabbath (arguably incorrectly), still seem to have no problem arranging diaries for pagan days of the week: Moon Day, Tiw's Day, Wodan's Day, Thor's day, Freya's Day and Saturn's Day. These trip off their tongues without any murmur of disapproval. So, I see rejection of Christmas as a misguided theological affectation.

Thirdly, and practically, is there any Christian benefit to having Christmas? I say: yes. Those jolly tribes-people in days of yore who gathered around the log fires were whistling in the dark that re-appeared every year in a cycle of hopeless repetition. They had no faith in a God of love who had everything under his charge, by Whom light could come into our hearts as well as our hearths, to conquer deadness forever.

An ancient story tells of a spiritual contest, held before the Saxon King Edwin, between Paulinus, a Christian missionary and pagan counsellors. The King, seated, listened as a pagan described what hope life held out in the old philosophy. The description by Bede of what his bleak world-view offered is very instructive for us now:

'When we compare the present life of man on earth to that time of which we have no knowledge, it seems to me like the swift flight of a single sparrow through the banqueting hall where you are sitting at dinner on a winter's day with your thanes and counsellors. In the midst there is a comforting fire to warm the hall; outside, the storms of winter rain or snow are raging. This sparrow flies swiftly in through one door of the hall, and out through another. While he is inside, he is safe from the winter storms; but after a few moments of comfort, he vanishes from sight into the wintry world from which he came. Even so, man appears on earth for a little while; but of what went before this life or of what follows, we know nothing.'

[Bede, Historia Ecclesiastica Gentis Anglorum, Book II, Chapter 13.]

Is it very surprising that the Saxon king chose an eternal Christian hope over cyclical pagan uncertainties?

The birth of Jesus, light of the world, could not have been more accurately substituted to fulfil the midwinter hopes of our ancestors: we Christians believe that Christ broke the cycle of death and temporary springtime with eternal life and love for all who will believe. We trust that, especially through Jesus, 'God is love.'

If you are raising a glass this midwinter festival by an evergreen tree, offer a toast to the anonymous genius who first thought of celebrating the midwinter festival in such a way as to proclaim Christ's everlasting victory over darkness, fear and death: the Day of the Unconquered Sun became the Day of the Unconquered Son.

So enjoy all the warmth, joy, friendships, presents and singing of this coming Christmas. But remember our ancestors needed something more, something lasting, something life-giving. I believe that this is found in Christ alone. Only He came to die for our sins, to set us free from slavery to selfishness and materialism, which binds us to our lower selves and offers us no higher freedom and escape than temporary oblivion.

23 December 2008

Religion 4

A piece of pure theatre

Kenneth Roy

At the place in the village where I wait for the bus in the morning, the daffodils are struggling to survive the Easter weekend. Battered by the wind and rain of the last week, they look half-dead already. The geese – thousands of them – who camped here over the winter, attracting the attention of bird-watchers from miles around, fled without warning. Suddenly, one morning, the field was lifeless again; I felt both deprived and sad. We are now looking forward to the swallows, whose arrival will announce the start of the real spring, not the bleak substitute we have been enduring. If the swallows ever failed to return, one senses it – the cycle of life – would be all over. We live in faith that they will.

All this is a mystery to me. Of course, like most other phenomena, it has been explained by science. But it remains a mystery. Science gives us explanations, not reasons.

Then there's us. Like flowers and migrating birds we too are a mystery without reasons. Tomorrow, if we're religious, and perhaps if we're not, we will be thinking about suffering and death and later in the weekend about an empty tomb and the great migration of the soul, whatever that is. I have never had the slightest difficulty about the Resurrection. It is so poetic, so fabulous an idea, such a piece of pure theatre, that even if it never occurred in quite the way the journalists of the day reported (for journalists usually get it wrong), it would still be worth celebrating. I refuse to think of churches as places for believers, many of whom are rather scary, some seriously dysfunctional. They are sanctuaries for all the troubled people of the world; somewhere to light a candle in the dark, metaphorically or actually. That is why the bolted doors of most churches for all but an hour on a Sunday is such an affront. We need them more when the believers aren't around.

There is the amusing question, this weekend as always, of

death and what happens then, if anything. I call it amusing, indeed it is vastly so, because it is the one question which has defied the ability of the greatest minds in the history of civilisation to answer. Think of them all: the scientists, the philosophers, the theologians, the physicists, the mathematicians, the politicians (on second thoughts let's leave that hopeless bunch out of it), the writers, the artists, and any other great minds that don't, for the moment, spring to mind. They have explained everything, rationalised the lot, and still they haven't sorted the one big question. One moment, poor little Jade Goody was alive; the next, dead. Where did she go? Nobody knows. All those seats of learning, millions of dissertations, countless conferences and summits, centuries of thought and speculation, and still we don't know what's happened to Jade Goody. If that isn't amusing, I don't know what is.

I have some atheist friends. On the whole they're a bit aggressive about their nihilism; so aggressive that I feel they must fear something. Being wrong, perhaps. How awful for these lovely people, immediately after their confidently predicted extinction, to be confronted by a retired male deity – I doubt that a woman would have been capable of such a mad scheme – who admits that he did indeed produce the Big Bang and then sat back to observe the dreadful results of his inspiration unfold before his disinterested eyes. Well, assuming the retired male deity has eyes. I don't suppose we can assume even that. The scientists haven't told us and I doubt that they ever will.

Life after death – with or without God – is one of those nice each-way bets rather than the rank outsider which won last Saturday's big race. What worries me more is the quality of this after-life. Such unscientific evidence as we have, including the testimony of spiritualists, not all of whom are cranks, suggests that the hereafter is a somewhat thin environment, an endless Scottish Sunday afternoon in winter, without curiosity or creativity, and that no one up there has the will or the energy to impart anything of the least interest or illumination. What, then, would be the point of this eternity? It would be worse than Airdrie. But what do I know? Like the Spanish waiter in *Fawlty*

Towers, I know nothing.

What's happened to Ian Mackenzie? Not long before he annoyed me by dying, I published his autobiography. Because I always think of him at Easter, as well as most other days, I reached for his book a moment ago and went straight to the ending. I haven't resolved a thing as I've written this, even to my own pathetic satisfaction, so I'll leave you this Easter with Ian Mackenzie:

At night, if I can't sleep, I sometimes go to the window and, if it is clear, look beyond the street lights to the space beyond. It becomes more and more difficult to get there, because earth's light pollution is blotting out the cosmos. But from the glebe fields by the Solway one can see the fields of stars. There they are, the revolving galaxies. Inside the cottage behind me is my little family which one of these days I will have to leave. But for now they're here to cherish. My heart beats for them, but my heart also reaches out to the family who left me, father, mother, Alan, Catherine, Etta. My heart reaches out so far it thins to invisibility. They, and my friends that have gone, have been travelling beyond death for years. They must have gone very far by now. I don't find words, but I yearn that somewhere in the mystery of universes, wherever they are, in whatever form they are, they could be touched by the unconditional love I feel for them.

The intensity passes. Is it real? Do they exist anywhere? How at one moment can one be surrounded by faith and see everything fit together, and at another moment feel so utterly lost in aloneness and unknowingness?

That uncertainty is how it has always been, and always must be, no doubt.

9 April 2009

Part XIII

And finally...

Diana's celestial boyfriend

And finally...

Diana's celestial boyfriend

Kenneth Roy

Although others will have noticed, two vigilant readers took the trouble to point out that, in last Thursday's column awarding two stars to the Scottish parliament, I prolonged the life of Diana, Princess of Wales, by almost two years, claiming that, at the time of the election of May 1999, she had just acquired a new boyfriend. My ever-watchful ex-colleague Marian Pallister and Professor John Izod tactfully pointed out that poor Diana was killed in August 1997, John putting it in these terms: 'Which [boyfriend] was that, Ken? I suspect in one of the few realms that escape the red tops'. Quite.

Three questions present themselves.

First, is it possible that, at the time of the devolution vote, Diana had indeed acquired a new boyfriend, albeit a celestial one? I have no knowledge of the theological position on relationships in the after-life; presumably no hankie-pankie permitted, the after-life being a place of unimpeachable virtue, but it would be interesting to have an official view of friendships in heaven – whether they are allowed and, if so, on what terms. By posing that first question, I think I was trying to dig myself out of a hole. I agree that it hasn't worked.

On quickly, then, to question 2. By dying in August 1997 rather than at some point in 1999 after the devolution vote, what did she miss? The devolution vote, for one thing, followed by Donald Dewar's marvellous speech. Anything else? The year before – 1998, unless I'm much mistaken, which of course I could be – she missed the Good Friday Agreement, the passing of the Human Rights Act giving 'a legal right to life' (coming too late for her), and the sending-off of David Beckham in the World Cup. The boy done bad, but it is remarkable looking back at the incident how Dave was blamed for just about everything wrong with England. Oh, and she missed the 43rd Eurovision Song Contest. It was held in Birmingham, England, that year and was won by a male-to-female transsexual called Dana. Not the sweet little thing from Ireland, the other Dana, who won it years before and who wasn't a male-to-female transsexual. No, no. From Israel, this one. Britain's Imaani was second. Whatever happened to Imaani? Where is she now? I would not care to speculate and, if I did, I'd probably get it wrong.

Looking back over the records of 1998 it occurs to me that, although we must have been quite excited about 1998 at the time, I mean as we lived through it, oohing and aahing at every new occurrence, in retrospect it is scarcely worth a row of beans, simply a succession of passing events. The truth is that Diana, Princess of Wales, did not miss very much, apart from her own life, of course. What was I myself doing in 1998? I have no specific memory of the year. It must have passed – like everything else.

I said there was a third question. There usually is. Oh, yes, I've remembered. How the hell could I have got that wrong? Tony Blair had only just been elected Prime Minister. We all loved him in those early days. He was so young and tall and, well, a little bit charismatic. We took his dramatic pauses seriously then. He had a gift for the gab. Then, shockingly, Diana died. Tony, with the help of Alastair Campbell, was the master of the moment, conjuring up the greatest soundbite in modern history, 'the People's Princess', out of the loose emotion lying around that Sunday morning. Later in the week, when the Queen was all over the place, or rather not all over the place but clinging on at Balmoral, and the public mood turned nasty, Tony sorted that too. Unlike David a year later, Tony done good. It made his premiership.

How could I have got it wrong? I was not in Scotland when I gave the Scottish parliament two cheers and prolonged the life of Diana, Princess of Wales. I was in a place called England, chairing a three-day conference, and maybe not thinking all that straight about dates and stuff, concerned as I was about the strange, closed world of the conference. The wind howled and the rain pattered down and there I sat, in front of a laptop early one morning, giving Diana another two precious years. How generous of me.

I believe, however, that this is only the second worst

inaccuracy of the year so far. A venerable columnist on the Spectator – I shall not name him because this man has said kind things about me in print more than once and you should never shop people who have been kind to you – claimed in January that the world was commemorating the 200th anniversary of the death of Robert Burns. That means, does it not, (you'll correct me if I've got this wrong too) that Robert died in 1809, so his life was prolonged by 13 years whereas I prolonged Diana, Princess of Wales's, by only two. I haven't bothered checking what, if anything, Robert missed in those 13 years, quite a lot of interest in France no doubt, but at least he was spared the Eurovision Song Contest and the World Cup.

Yet, as the perpetrator of the second worst inaccuracy of the year so far, I am worried – obviously. I find myself in the embarrassing position of one of those MPs who, having claimed quite properly for only £230,363 in second home allowances, inadvertently applied to the fees office for the cost of a Kit-Kat. How could they have got it so wrong? How could I? I may have to stick to duff predictions in future.

12 March 2009

Notes on contributors

Kenneth Roy has been editor of the Scottish Review (in print and online) since its foundation in 1995. He is founder of the Institute of Contemporary Scotland and of the Young UK and Ireland Programme

Walter Humes is research professor in education at the University of the West of Scotland and former professor of education at the University of Aberdeen

Alan McIntyre is a Scottish-born partner in a New York-based financial services company

Gordon MacGregor is a postgraduate law student

Islay McLeod is assistant editor of the Scottish Review and assistant director of the Institute of Contemporary Scotland

Jock Gallagher, a former senior BBC executive, is director of the Centre for Media Freedom attached to the University of Sheffield

Alex Wood is a secondary head teacher in Edinburgh and a former Edinburgh district councillor

R D Kernohan is a journalist, writer and broadcaster. He is a former editor of Life and Work, the magazine of the Church of Scotland

Andrew Hook is a former professor of English literature at the University of Glasgow and the author/editor of many books on literary subjects

Alan Fisher is an Al Jazeera correspondent and a much-travelled reporter

Catherine Czerkawska is a novelist and playwright

Barbara Millar is a freelance journalist and tour guide

P J B Slater is emeritus professor of natural history at the University of St Andrews and past president of the Association for the Study of Animal Behaviour

Ian Mackay is a chartered accountant, an honorary sheriff and a champion curler

Sheila Hetherington is the author of *Katharine Atholl, Against the Tide*, the biography of the first woman to have been a Conservative minister

Robins Millar (1889-1968) was a leading Scottish journalist – editor of the Evening News in Glasgow, theatre critic of the Scottish Daily Express. He was also a successful playwright

Bruce Gardner is a Church of Scotland minister and former teacher